PITCH YOUR POTENTIAL

PITCH
YOUR
POTENTIAL

VICKI JOHNSON, Ph.D.

PITCH YOUR POTENTIAL

THE FORMULA FOR WINNING DREAM JOBS, AWARDS, AND ELITE OPPORTUNITIES

WILEY

Copyright © 2026 by John Wiley & Sons. All rights reserved, including rights for text and data mining and training of artificial intelligence technologies or similar technologies.

Published by John Wiley & Sons, Inc., Hoboken, New Jersey.

No part of this publication may be reproduced, stored in a retrieval system, or transmitted in any form or by any means, electronic, mechanical, photocopying, recording, scanning, or otherwise, except as permitted under Section 107 or 108 of the 1976 United States Copyright Act, without either the prior written permission of the Publisher, or authorization through payment of the appropriate per-copy fee to the Copyright Clearance Center, Inc., 222 Rosewood Drive, Danvers, MA 01923, (978) 750-8400, fax (978) 750-4470, or on the web at www.copyright.com. Requests to the Publisher for permission should be addressed to the Permissions Department, John Wiley & Sons, Inc., 111 River Street, Hoboken, NJ 07030, (201) 748-6011, fax (201) 748-6008, or online at http://www.wiley.com/go/permission.

The manufacturer's authorized representative according to the EU General Product Safety Regulation is Wiley-VCH GmbH, Boschstr. 12, 69469 Weinheim, Germany, e-mail: Product_Safety@wiley.com.

Trademarks: Wiley and the Wiley logo are trademarks or registered trademarks of John Wiley & Sons, Inc. and/or its affiliates in the United States and other countries and may not be used without written permission. All other trademarks are the property of their respective owners. John Wiley & Sons, Inc. is not associated with any product or vendor mentioned in this book.

Limit of Liability/Disclaimer of Warranty: While the publisher and the authors have used their best efforts in preparing this work, including a review of the content of the work, neither the publisher nor the authors make any representations or warranties with respect to the accuracy or completeness of the contents of this work and specifically disclaim all warranties, including without limitation any implied warranties of merchantability or fitness for a particular purpose. Certain AI systems have been used in the creation of this work. No warranty may be created or extended by sales representatives, written sales materials or promotional statements for this work. The fact that an organization, website, or product is referred to in this work as a citation and/or potential source of further information does not mean that the publisher and authors endorse the information or services the organization, website, or product may provide or recommendations it may make. This work is sold with the understanding that the publisher is not engaged in rendering professional services. The advice and strategies contained herein may not be suitable for your situation. You should consult with a specialist where appropriate. Further, readers should be aware that websites listed in this work may have changed or disappeared between when this work was written and when it is read. Neither the publisher nor authors shall be liable for any loss of profit or any other commercial damages, including but not limited to special, incidental, consequential, or other damages.

For general information on our other products and services or for technical support, please contact our Customer Care Department within the United States at (800) 762-2974, outside the United States at (317) 572-3993 or fax (317) 572-4002.

Wiley also publishes its books in a variety of electronic formats. Some content that appears in print may not be available in electronic formats. For more information about Wiley products, visit our web site at www.wiley.com.

Library of Congress Cataloging-in-Publication Data is Available:

ISBN 9781394328260 (Cloth)
ISBN 9781394328277 (ePub)
ISBN 9781394328284 (ePDF)

Cover Design: Wiley
Author Photo: Courtesy of Hillary Jeanne Photography
SKY10134858_121725

To Ryan, who has always seen my potential long before I see it in myself

Contents

Introduction	xi
Chapter 1 Build Your Winner's Mindset: Prepare with Confidence, Compete Without Fear	1
Embrace Your Fear of Failure and Rejection	8
Negate the Impact of Gatekeepers	12
Deliberate Gatekeeping	12
Well-Intentioned Gatekeeping	14
Listen to Guides, Not Gatekeepers	16
Lower Your Fear of Comparison	19
Develop Your Winner's Mindset	22
It's Not a Numbers Game	22
The Advantage of Authentic Desire	23
Writing a Compelling Personal Pitch	25
Your Winning Application Story	26
The MATCH ME Formula®	28
Key Takeaways	30
How to Use This Book	31
Chapter 2 Become **Memorable:** Stick in the Minds of the Selection Committee	33
Why Being Memorable Matters	35

Five Factors of Positive Memorability	37
Get a Referral from a Mutual Contact	39
Make a Self-Introduction to a Selector	43
Propose a Memorable Idea	48
Use Memorable Anecdotes from Your Life	51
Start Practicing	54
Key Takeaways	55
Your Turn	56

Chapter 3 **Align** Your Mission with Theirs: Win Trust by Championing Their Cause — 57

Why Mission Alignment Matters	61
What the Organization's Mission Is	63
What the Organization's Mission Is Not	64
How to Demonstrate Mission Alignment	65
Research the Organization's Mission	66
Define Your Personal Mission	73
Show Mission Alignment	76
Your Personal Mission Is a Journey, Not a Destination	79
Key Takeaways	80
Your Turn	81

Chapter 4 Make Your Goals **Timely:** Prove Your Impact Can't Wait — 83

Why Timeliness Matters	85
Demonstrate Timeliness by Incorporating Current Events	86
Demonstrate Timeliness Through Urgency	92
Key Takeaways	96
Your Turn	96

Contents

Chapter 5 **Capitalize** on the Organization's Unique Benefits: Turn Their Brag Points into Your Bonus Points — 97
  Why Capitalizing on the Organization's Unique Benefits Matters — 101
  How to Find the Organization's Unique Benefits — 103
  Ways to Capitalize on the Organization's Unique Benefits — 106
  Make the Organization the "Hero" of Your Application Story — 110
  Key Takeaways — 117
  Your Turn — 118

Chapter 6 Be **Highly Specific:** Use Detail That Captivates Selectors — 119
  Why Specificity and Detail Matter — 124
  Replace Platitudes and Jargon — 125
    Adding Words for Greater Specificity — 127
    Removing Words for Greater Specificity — 128
  Create a Highly Specific Career Goal — 129
    The MATCH ME Career Goal — 130
    When You Don't Have a Specific Career Goal — 135
  Proposing Highly Specific Projects — 136
  Obtain Highly Specific References — 140
  Key Takeaways — 142
  Your Turn — 143

Chapter 7 Make Your Pitch **Mutually Beneficial:** Show How You Win When They Win — 145
  Why Mutual Benefit Matters — 150
  How to Express Your Personal Needs — 152
    Define Your Need for Financial Benefits — 153
    Express Your Need for Educational Benefits — 157
    Show Your Need for Network Benefits — 158

	Paying the Benefits Forward	161
	Key Takeaways	163
	Your Turn	164
Chapter 8	Master **Elegance:** Balance Your Tone with Self-Confidence and Humility	165
	What Elegance Is and Why It Matters	169
	How a Winner's Mindset Creates Elegance	171
	Nix Calling Yourself the "Best" Candidate	173
	Recognize That Accomplishments Are Evidence, Not Self-Praise	175
	Have Empathy for Your Selectors	177
	Key Takeaways	179
	Your Turn	179
Chapter 9	Apply the MATCH ME Formula®: Put the Full Formula to Work in Your Pitch	181
	How to Create Your Winning Application Story	184
	Three Frameworks to Help You Apply the MATCH ME Formula®	187
	A MATCH ME Formula® Cover Letter	188
	A MATCH ME Formula® Personal Statement	192
	MATCH ME Formula® Interview Prep	200
	Guiding Questions to Apply the MATCH ME Formula®	206
	We Believe in You	207

References	*209*
Work with Me	*213*
Acknowledgments	*215*
About the Author	*219*
Index	*221*

Introduction

Competition with our peers begins in childhood, but the real stakes begin in adolescence when we apply to college and prepare for our future careers, without any certainty of what adulthood has in store for us.

But there is one thing you can be certain of: you will be asked many times why you should be selected from among tens to thousands of other candidates—when applying to universities, to jobs, and for awards, and when pitching yourself for promotions and special opportunities.

The competitive process of applying and advocating for your selection will inevitably trigger your deepest fears that you are not good enough to be chosen for the opportunities you have your heart set on. But this fear is just the result of not having a framework to compellingly answer the question "Why you?" Because we are not taught an effective framework in grade school or college, we apply an idea of what might work and are left to wonder why it sometimes works but often fails.

We live in a society that feeds the narrative that only people with special connections, money, or a high IQ can achieve elite opportunities. Yet there are always examples of people without these things who were selected against the odds. This is because there are strategies for creating a winning application that anyone can apply, no matter your upbringing, financial status, or degree of success until now.

I learned this approach through experimentation. By leveraging the one thing that is truly unique to me—my lived experience—I turned the story of my future potential into my most powerful competitive advantage. Today, I love teaching this mastery to others.

My Story

I was born in Philadelphia in 1979 and from age four was raised in a rowhouse in Wilmington, Delaware, where my siblings and I attended city public schools. I had the privilege of being lovingly raised by two parents: my father, a Lutheran minister, and my mother, a nurse, who stayed at home when my siblings and I were young. In my adolescence, I learned important values and life skills from my parents, including the art of storytelling from my father, who is an experienced writer and speaker, and the power of attention to detail from my mother, who made our home beautiful despite having limited resources.

From a young age, I loved school and had a personal ambition to become a leader. Influenced by family and mentors who valued serving others, I also had a desire to work in public service. I discovered who I am and what my purpose is by setting high goals and pursuing them with the determination of an explorer. I've always operated with the optimism that even when I failed, I would gain skills in the process and get selected for the right opportunities that were meant for me.

I made the most of every educational opportunity I had available to me, and when I was a high school senior in 1997, I was college-bound. But I had some obstacles to achieving my dream of attending an Ivy League university. As you'll learn later in this book, I successfully used the power of story and other human-centered strategies to get selected for the 2001 class of Cornell University with a substantial financial aid package. This early success of overcoming the odds of failure was a catalyst for my self-confidence. It was a signal that I had the potential to achieve much more, and I listened to this signal.

I was, however, challenged by one thing throughout my career: I constantly received advice from others to lower my goals and expectations because, from their perspective, my academic record and résumé were not good enough to rival my competitors. I regularly received the message from mentors that I should pursue less competitive opportunities where I had a higher probability of success. Even as I achieved success, the competition loomed bigger at every stage in my career, and the message that I should have a plan B never waned.

But I experimented with storytelling tactics and applied to many exciting opportunities anyway, because my goal was to have a career adventure. I wanted to make a social impact, travel the world, do exciting work, and become a leader in my field, whatever that field would be. I know many of you reading this book share these same goals.

From college, I had my eye on several prestigious professional fellowships in the United States and abroad that would help me enter and advance my early career in public health and emergency management. Each fellowship had a monthslong application process requiring a personal essay or project proposal, recommendation letters, and a finalist interview. When I first started applying for these my senior year in college, my senior advisor, a distinguished professor, commented that these nationally competitive awards "might be a waste of my time" because of my 3.2 GPA and lack of internships.

I took my advisor's feedback with a grain of salt and focused on being the most prepared applicant. This commitment paid off over the next decade of my career, not just because I was ultimately successful winning several nationally competitive fellowships but also because I developed a specialized skill in persuasive communications: the personal pitch. The fellowships I achieved included the New York City Urban Fellows Program (2001); a German Chancellor Fellowship in Germany (2003); the Herbert Scoville Jr. Peace Fellowship in

Washington, DC (2005); and the Ian Axford Fellowship in Public Policy (2011), a midcareer Fulbright award offered in New Zealand. In all of these fellowship competitions, there were competitors who had better résumés, more experience, and more credentials than I did, so winning these fellowships signaled to me I was doing something right in my applications.

Throughout my early career, I kept honing my personal pitch by using the story of my potential as my greatest competitive edge. At the age of 30, I landed a dream job within President Barack Obama's administration. I was selected to become the policy director of the National Commission on Children and Disasters, an expert body instituted by Congress in response to the outcomes of Hurricane Katrina. The policy director job was a sought-after role, responsible for leading the incorporation and analysis of input from 10 expert commissioners, nationally selected from a range of disciplines, as well as input from hundreds of external experts and stakeholder organizations. It was an aspirational leadership role, and many people advised that I would not be qualified for it, but I applied anyway, getting my foot in the door through a referral from my network. Through intense preparation, which I talk about in Chapter 6, I ultimately edged out several impressive candidates with congressional experience, doctorates, and 10–20 years more work experience. Worried about how my age would be perceived once I entered the role, I worked hard to prove that I deserved the job, and my effort was acknowledged. After submitting our final report to Congress, I received a standing ovation for my orchestration of the final report from a room that included the commissioners and many federal leaders.

On the academic side, I had success getting accepted into top graduate schools and went on to earn my Master of Science in Public Health at the London School of Hygiene & Tropical Medicine, the leading public health school in Europe. In my mid-30s, I undertook my Ph.D. at Massey University in New Zealand at the encouragement of Kiwi professor Dr. David Johnston, whom I met during my

Fulbright work. Although I didn't need a doctorate for my career track, I enjoyed research and had a skill for it. I saw the unexpected opportunity as part of my career adventure because it was fully funded, and it allowed my husband, Ryan, and me to extend our time abroad.

Dr. Johnston served as my graduate advisor, and I took advantage of the positive support he offered. He was the first academic advisor I ever had who fully believed in what I could achieve, not just academically but also personally and professionally. With the vote of confidence that I had desired my whole life, I worked exceptionally hard and transformed from being a B-average student to a Ph.D. recipient who won the Dean's Award for Exceptional Theses, placing me in the top 10% of all Ph.D. recipients at the university. I finally reached my full academic potential. Dr. Johnston's positive support was a secret ingredient to my success that strongly influenced how I mentor others today.

In 2011, while I was a Ph.D. student in New Zealand, Ryan and I also co-founded ProFellow®, an information platform for people seeking fellowships and other merit-based funding awards. I am blessed to be married to my biggest fan, who saw my potential as an entrepreneur. Ryan came up with the idea for ProFellow after seeing me speak on fellowships and the excited reception I received from the young women professionals who attended. We entered many business plan and pitch competitions, which were experiences new to me, but they helped me further hone my skills in developing a winning application story. In several of the competitions, we received first place!

But, as a business, ProFellow was not an instant success. It was a passion project for the first five years. The reason ProFellow exists today is that we didn't give up. Our commitment to our mission to make funding opportunities more accessible was the ultimate reason ProFellow lasted and gained ground during a period when many other similar companies started and failed.

From New Zealand, we moved to San Francisco, and two years after completing my Ph.D., I made a major career change from working in public policy to working full-time as an entrepreneur. In 2016, I resigned from my last full-time policy job at the San Francisco Public Utilities Commission, where I became disillusioned after witnessing corruption. It was a huge risk to leave my career ladder in government, especially because the pay was good and we were new parents living in a very expensive city. But Ryan and I wanted to give the ProFellow idea a real chance to succeed.

We decided I would focus full-time on ProFellow for at least one year with fellowship advertising as our business model. To make this financially possible, we sold our only car and decided to stay put in our one-bedroom apartment through the birth of our second child. Building a company while living in a cramped apartment with two children under the age of three was an adventure in itself (and many friends and family had opinions about this lifestyle choice), but the sacrifice was worth it. Due to the strong web traffic and reputation ProFellow had gained organically over the previous five years, the company grew, and I was able to replace my previous government salary within two years. I am certain it would not have been successful without the groundwork that had been laid years before, reminding me of the importance of commitment and early preparation.

In 2018, I was selected for the Nasdaq Entrepreneurial Center's Milestone Makers program, a globally competitive business accelerator in San Francisco, the heart of Silicon Valley. With this program as a launchpad, I explored new revenue streams. I created ProFellow's Fully Funded Course and Mentorship Program, a highly successful online course and group coaching program that in five years, with a team of me and one part-time coach, helped more than 300 candidates enter highly competitive, fully funded Ph.D. and master's programs and national fellowships. The participants collectively won more than $36 million in merit-based graduate funding. The delivery of effective online courses for applicants skyrocketed ProFellow's success and was the start of my work as a public speaker and trainer.

After building and sustaining a mission-driven business, my aspirations continued to climb. The creation of this book, chosen and supported by Wiley, is also a major milestone in my career adventure. I am now an author and speaker and have the opportunity to share my unique talents with individuals and organizations all over the world.

How the MATCH ME Formula® Was Born

Applying successfully to competitive opportunities had become easier for me, not because I had more accomplishments to bolster my résumé, but because, through practice, I had become more attuned to what works and what doesn't when answering the question "Why you?" I also had become more adaptable and creative as I made career changes from government to academia to business, each time starting from ground zero in regard to the level of experience I had in each industry.

Early in my career, I could not articulate what I was doing differently from my peers when I achieved opportunities that others assumed I had no chance of winning. As I became more experienced in my approach, I began to reflect on my strategies for success and began sharing them through individual mentorship. When those I mentored started to achieve extraordinary success too, I realized I could teach my application approach to larger audiences, especially those who have historically faced obstacles, and help level the playing field.

Throughout my work with ProFellow, now a leading media platform for merit-based awards, accelerators, and academic opportunities, I have taught thousands of people how to become a top contender for the world's most competitive opportunities.

To communicate the strategies I teach, I created the MATCH ME Formula®. Each letter of MATCH ME represents the seven elements of a winning application. A winning application is: *Memorable*; *Aligns with the organization's mission*; *Timely*; *Capitalizes on the organization's unique benefits*; *Highly specific*; *Mutually beneficial*; and *Elegant*.

The MATCH ME Formula® is a framework for how to communicate your application story with a compelling vision of your future potential—in other words, how to effectively answer the question "Why you?" in application essays, cover letters, interviews, pitches, and negotiations. It's a formula that virtually anyone, from any background or upbringing, can apply because it leverages knowledge and tools that everyone has access to.

The MATCH ME Formula® has been tested for more than 10 years through courses, workshops, and mentorship programs that I have delivered through ProFellow, universities, and the corporate sector. In particular, I have taught this formula to groups that struggle the most with gatekeeping, comparison culture, and impostor syndrome. You'll have an opportunity in this book to meet real people who have used the MATCH ME Formula® to achieve extraordinary success.

I hope you'll have an open mind as you learn the MATCH ME Formula® and begin applying it to each competitive opportunity you choose. Please share your results with me! I look forward to hearing about your career adventure.

1 | Build Your Winner's Mindset

Prepare with Confidence, Compete Without Fear

No amount of external validation will surpass the power of your own self-belief. It is not other people's encouragement, but your self-confidence and courage that dictate how hard you will work to achieve a goal. Throughout your career, you're going to face messaging that will cause you to doubt your skills, talents, and ideas. But as you receive career advice and feedback from others, it's important to recognize that the widely held belief that the competition is fierce—for jobs, for top university spots, for awards, and for recognition—is simply an idea that stems from a collection of our own individual fears about what we can and can't achieve. Yet, the competition doesn't determine what you are capable of—only your actions do.

Throughout my life—from attending under-resourced public schools to working in male-dominated sectors such as emergency management, higher education, and business—I found that many people won't take you seriously based on factors beyond your control. When I was young, I wanted badly to be taken seriously, but I was discouraged by the advice and feedback I received as I dreamed about college and a successful career. But one selection committee can change your life's trajectory by choosing you. Their selection will also change the way you think about yourself and what you are capable of. When you recognize that you can capture a dream opportunity by inspiring selectors with your story, you will understand why the story of your future potential is so important to create, cultivate, practice, and share. However, to create and share a story that ignites emotion and compels others to invest in you, you must believe that you determine your own future and enter the competitions of your career with confidence and without fear. I wrote this book to show you how, through applying the MATCH ME Formula®.

The MATCH ME Formula® had its beginnings early in my life when I entered the first big competition of my career: applying to college. At 17 years old, I was hardworking and ambitious and ready to make my mark on the world. My goal was to get into Cornell University, the Ivy League university my dad attended in the late 1960s. But I would take a different path than my dad, who, inspired by the Civil Rights Movement, decided to leave engineering to work in the inner city as a Lutheran minister, giving up financial success for religious purpose. My dream was to work in public service at the highest level and achieve greater financial security than my parents had, and I felt an elite college degree would help me do just that. I needed not just an acceptance to a top school but also enough financial aid to make attendance possible.

Applying to college was the beginning of my education on how to pitch my potential to selection committees. The competition for a spot at an Ivy League university is one few are truly prepared for, and the adults in my life made this reality very clear. My parents didn't discourage me, but they strongly encouraged me to apply to less competitive, local schools like the University of Delaware. With the rise of mailer and Internet marketing in the 1990s, the number of applications to Cornell increased to more than 20,000 per year, and the expectations of candidates were much higher than when my dad attended.

Since there was no family pressure to apply to Cornell, I initially had very little knowledge of the university and no interest in applying. But my dad suggested we visit the Cornell campus in Ithaca, New York, as a last-minute side excursion while we road-tripped for a campus tour at nearby Syracuse University. This unexpected detour changed my college goals. I immediately fell in love with the beautiful Cornell campus floating high above Lake Cayuga, which my dad described for years as desperately cold and hilly. It felt like home when I walked through the Arts & Sciences quad for the first time, and this unexplained feeling caused me to believe I was meant to be there. When I became emphatic about applying, my dad gave me hesitant support. I sensed he was afraid I would get my hopes up, about both acceptance and financial aid.

Surprisingly, the biggest challenge applying to Cornell was not the effort required to apply but the discouraging feedback I received from others in the process. Whenever I have had a big, aspirational goal, I've had someone or something remind me of the probability of my failure based on the number and caliber of people I would be up against.

My first high-stakes encounter with failure rates was in a meeting with my high school guidance counselor in 1996. We met in her cramped office to discuss my plans to apply to college, including my dream school, Cornell. I was tense and excited, waiting for her enthusiastic nod of support. She quietly looked over my report card and combined SAT score, a small frown forming on her face.

"Your 1250 SAT score is not a bad score, but let's not get too excited about Cornell," she said. "Cornell has a very low acceptance rate, which means most applicants don't get in. Your SAT score is not even in the ballpark of the type of students who go to Cornell. Make sure you include safety schools on your list." She looked up at me pointedly over her eyeglasses.

Her message was loud and clear: *you don't stack up to the competition.* Does this scene sound familiar to you?

It's true that in applying to Cornell, I had a lot of compensating to do. I had straight As but was attending a failing city public high school that offered only a few AP classes. I was a Girl Scout Gold Award recipient and a leader in virtually every extracurricular activity I joined: senior class president, field hockey captain, and drum major of the high school marching band. Problem? None of my high school groups rivaled others in the state. Then there was my 1250 SAT score. Not a bad score, but possibly too low to make me an Ivy League contender. I also lacked college admissions coaching and had no examples from my high school of graduates who had gone on to Ivy League universities.

I did have "legacy" status from my dad, which I thought could be a big advantage, but I was told this might give me only a slight advantage over applicants with similar credentials.

Despite the odds of being rejected, I resolved to apply and committed to being the most prepared applicant I could be, given the resources available to me. I prepared by researching what Cornell was looking for in candidates and reflecting deeply on what I had to offer in alignment with their mission. I was so obsessed with my goal that I worked on it daily.

In looking for insider information about the selection committee, I didn't have much to work from. The Internet wasn't much help back then. So for weeks I scrutinized Cornell's marketing brochures to spark ideas for my personal statement story. I took detailed notes on their brag points, like the student body's economic diversity and a statement about how Cornell develops future leaders. I read articles about notable women alumnae in public service, like Ruth Bader Ginsburg and Janet Reno.

During this period, I would sometimes stay up late, while my little sister Katie slept quietly in the bed beside me, and dream with my eyes open.

I envisioned the Cornell selection committee in a poorly lit conference room, reading paper copies of hundreds of personal statements from applicants all over the world.

"Oh gee, another state champion," one woman in a cardigan would say, rolling her eyes. "Did you read this one?" said a graying professor in a tweed jacket. "She has a 1600 SAT score and spent a summer in Bali saving the white rhinoceros!" The sarcasm was thickening. They were tired and bored.

"Hold on . . . you've got to read this one!" said a professor in Harry Potter glasses, standing in surprise.

In this daydream, he was holding up my personal statement, and that statement was telling a story that stood out from the competition.

What was in it? I didn't immediately know. I wished my active imagination would help me here.

I did, however, have a unique strength as a young person: I understood the power of story. I knew that if I could identify what drives the selection committee's decision-making and tell an aligned and compelling story about my lived experience, goals, and future potential in my personal statement, my Cornell application would stand out in a sea of other "average" candidates for a coveted spot at the university.

With my writer's block mounting, I shared some essay ideas with my dad.

"Why not tell them what it's like to be captain of the state's worst high school field hockey team?" he said.

A lightbulb went off.

See, my dad is a master storyteller. From early childhood, I watched him give hundreds of sermons telling human stories that deeply moved his congregation from compassion to laughter to tears. I didn't know it at the time, but I had become an apprentice to his storytelling skills. This is why his essay idea immediately made sense to me.

After many edits, I finished my personal statement, which shared my story of what it was like to be captain of a team with the worst losing streak in the state of Delaware. I expressed my experience with daily practice, ambition, disappointment, teamwork, and friendship. In other parts of my application, I linked this experience to my career goal to become a leader in public service, applying my higher education at Cornell to social impact that would reflect my values.

Only years later could I articulate what was so powerful about this personal statement. The story of my unique lived experience was different from the majority of essays about success and achievement from privileged applicants and the essays about personal struggle from less privileged applicants. More importantly, it expressed a multitude of messages in just a few lines. Without saying it directly, the story demonstrated my leadership skills, strong personal drive, intellect, maturity, and commitment to others, the key factors that Cornell looks for in applicants. It also hinted at my high school's resource constraints and my family's economic challenges, helping to explain the shortcomings in my SAT score.

I got in, and I received almost a full ride in financial aid. It was a dream come true. To this day, I'll never forget the feeling of achievement when I opened my Cornell acceptance letter. It lit a fire in me to always listen to my intuition and strive for the biggest goals I have my heart set on, no matter what.

There is no way to know exactly why I was selected over other candidates. I felt extraordinarily fortunate to be selected by Cornell, and I wondered if my legacy status played a major role.

But, while making friends at Cornell, some of whom went to elite private high schools, I was surprised to learn that there were Cornell legacy applicants from their high schools who did not get into Cornell. Also, my parents weren't donors, and I required significant financial aid to attend, so there was no financial incentive for selecting me.

These points helped me consider objectively all the factors from my application that likely contributed to my success.

Having studied the art of preparing a winning application, I now believe that my story had a major impact on my selection. It helped me stand out among candidates who had great accomplishments but lacked the important ingredients I offered in my application story like mission alignment, reciprocity, authentic desire, and a future vision of positive impact on others. I had begun to crack the code on how to pitch my potential to achieve extraordinary success. But it would be many years before I recognized this and understood why my story approach worked.

In any case, I did not take my acceptance to Cornell for granted. I did everything in my power to make the most of the assets that Cornell provided me toward building a career in social impact, first working for 15 years in public health and emergency management and later founding ProFellow® to help others access opportunities. I believe the Cornell selectors saw this potential in me because of my application story.

My acceptance to Cornell was the catalyst for a life-changing realization that all forms of advice about how to achieve personal goals are subjective and limited by what the mentor does not know. Surprising to me, this experience of being advised that I didn't stack up to the competition happened to me over and over again throughout my life, despite my increasing record of achievement. Every time I applied to highly competitive jobs, fellowships, graduate schools, and leadership opportunities, and when I became an entrepreneur founding my own company, other people advised me to lower my goals and expectations because of the competition I would be up against.

Rather than allow this discouragement to fuel my self-doubt, I developed the mindset early on that I can take career advice and separate it from the truth of what I am truly capable of. I resolved not to allow others' opinions of my probability of failure to stop me from pursuing big goals. I focused obsessively on being the most prepared applicant in the competition and proving that I deserved the opportunity.

I call this mentality the *winner's mindset*.

Once I learned that the story of my future is more important to selectors than the story of my past, I sought to become a master at painting a compelling vision of my future potential. I honed several specialized skills in investigative research, persuasive writing, speaking, and negotiation that have helped me to become an exceptional applicant in any competition I entered. Later in my career, when others began to come to me for career and application advice, I realized I had the ability to teach these skills to others and provide the positive encouragement I never had.

Even with exceptional communication skills, you can face mindset challenges that can hold you back from applying these skills successfully. Before I get into the seven elements of the MATCH ME Formula®, I want you to gain a better understanding of the mental roadblocks you face when applying to elite opportunities that seem out of reach, and how to overcome their negative effects.

Embrace Your Fear of Failure and Rejection

From a young age, I grew up with the sense that failure and rejection—and even just the possibility of failure—are things we should be ashamed of and hide, as if it is possible to have a perfect record of success. I was trained not to broadcast my rejections and failures, and so like most people, I have a public bio and résumé that highlight only my accomplishments. Even when I wrote the first draft of this book, I didn't mention my experience with rejections out of ingrained habit.

For the record, there are many jobs, universities, awards, and fellowships that I applied to that resulted in a "No" or, worse, no response at all. Despite grappling with my disappointment, I learned from each and every one of these rejections. Through these experiences, I learned that my fear of rejection is a powerful sixth sense that would help me identify the right opportunities for me. However, I had to resist the urge to suppress this uncomfortable feeling, as we're often taught.

Some influencers today speak about ways to reduce the degree of emotional pain people experience from rejections, and this content has become hugely popular. One of the most popular TED talks of all time, with more than 10 million views, is Jia Jiang's "What I Learned from 100 Days of Rejection" (Jiang 2016). Jiang suggests that we can become more courageous by regularly experimenting with asking for things. Jiang spent 100 days asking strangers for odd favors. Most things he asked for were weird requests like a "burger refill" at a restaurant—requests he assumed would result in a "No." This practice helped him become more accustomed to and less emotional about rejection. In some cases, he received a "Yes," which surprised him. He also started asking for feedback when people said "No," which allowed him to learn the real reasons behind the responses rather than make assumptions, which turned out to be a great learning experience.

But the problem with how Jiang aimed to desensitize rejection is that he asked strangers for things that he did not authentically desire. While strengthening courage is a step in the right direction, I don't think this approach is the right practice for achieving the things that you do want, because emotion is removed not just from the outcome but also from the ask. This type of practice trains our brains to work less hard when we compete, like the "spray and pray" approach: superficially applying to lots of opportunities at once in the hope that at least one will land.

Our minds and bodies are designed to help us recognize and avoid threats that cause both physical and emotional pain. When there is an opportunity that you truly desire, your adrenaline spikes. Your body recognizes the stakes are high, and your mind starts working in overdrive. The fear of not achieving that opportunity can either prompt you to put in your absolute best effort to improve your chance of achievement (increase positive feelings) or avoid the pain of unrewarded effort (decrease negative feelings). Usually, we lean toward avoiding pain because we assume that rejection is more likely than success. Our minds subconsciously try to reduce the expected pain by reducing the effort to achieve the goal through tactics like procrastination or avoiding the effort altogether.

To be successful, we need to train our minds to do the opposite: we need to allow fear to help us recognize great opportunities as valuable and lean in emotionally on the possibility of success so we try harder. We need to stop telling ourselves and others that we don't expect to get selected just to preempt our disappointment.

Of course, the winner's mindset doesn't address the fact that some opportunities are controlled by different forms of discrimination that cause unfair rejections and glass ceilings. Many people are held back from pursuing elite opportunities due to their fear of discrimination, and perhaps that is exactly what these barriers are designed to achieve.

But when we harden a mental narrative that we are predetermined to fail, it's unlikely we will learn from the process and take personal responsibility for a rejection. This negative mindset narrows our ability to see and access the abundance of opportunities that exist to achieve our goals.

The key is to be intentional and focus on the many opportunities where your candidacy is welcome and use these opportunities to advance into a leadership position where you can create opportunities for yourself and others. We don't have to join the ranks of the people who maintain unfair barriers. We can create new spheres of influence and power as inclusive leaders by building skills, resources, and networks. To do this, we must reframe how we view success and failure as we pursue opportunities today.

In reflecting on my rejections from top jobs and university spots, the things that I did not get chosen for were opportunities that I was not fully aligned with. I did not pitch a compelling vision of my future potential because I didn't yet have the skills or ideas needed to stand out among the competition or I did not apply my best effort to the application or both. In all cases where I didn't apply my best effort, there was a mindset challenge that was holding me back from giving it my all. Some of my applications to opportunities were driven by a sense of what I *should* do, fueled by society's pressure to climb a career ladder and chase progressively higher titles and pay, rather than what I wanted to do based on my interests. Nonetheless, I gained something from every single one of these applications, including the opportunity to practice persuasive communication skills and better define my personal mission. Applying to competitive opportunities also helped me build the deep professional network I have today.

Rejections also prompted me to be much more selective in what I apply to, but without lowering my high goals. I focused on quality applications over quantity and reminded myself of what I had to gain from each competition I entered. In time, I found my zone of genius: I have a unique knack for identifying exactly what selection committees are looking for, choosing highly aligned opportunities, and carefully and creatively tailoring my application story to each opportunity.

I believe we should leverage our emotional fear of failure to work harder and refuse to be ashamed of rejection. This puts the power back in your hands and helps you overcome mindset challenges that prevent you from putting your best foot forward. Whenever I believed in my possibility of success and put my absolute best effort into the application, ironically, it became easier for me to let go of the outcome, because I was proud of the quality of what I submitted.

Many people I have mentored shared with me that they experienced this same feeling after applying the strategies I teach. Rather than feeling worried about their performance in a job or university application as they awaited the result, they felt great pride and a release of fear, which is an incredible outcome by itself. Many of these applicants built stronger relationships with the people who served as references and the people on the selection committee because these witnesses were incredibly impressed with their high effort. This observation is the foundation of a mantra I repeat often.

There is no such thing as unrewarded effort when you apply your greatest effort. Even if you don't get the opportunity, the selectors and those who recommend you are seeing you in the best way possible. This builds your professional network and reputation and pays off in opportunities that come to you in the future in ways that you can't imagine in the moment.

The lesson is, you can only control your input, so create something you are proud of every single time.

Negate the Impact of Gatekeepers

Another mental barrier comes from gatekeeping. In my experience working with thousands of students and professionals, I found that many talented people have an inner belief that they are below average among their peers despite their strong record of achievement. My theory is that this inner belief stems from a mentor's discouragement when you sought to pursue a high goal—what I refer to as *gatekeeping*. Gatekeeping is an additional hurdle that you need to overcome before you've even made the decision to compete.

Getting into Cornell was my first success in overcoming the discouragement of an academic gatekeeper, my guidance counselor. This early life experience demonstrated to me that all forms of advice, mentorship, and guidance are opinions, not facts. After achieving my first big goal, I realized that if I had agreed with my guidance counselor's assessment and self-selected out of applying to Cornell, my life would have been on a very different trajectory. Worse, I would have had no idea that I missed my opportunity.

There are two types of gatekeeping: deliberate and well-intentioned.

Deliberate Gatekeeping

Deliberate gatekeeping is applied by self-interested people who aim to maintain the status quo of influence and access among certain privileged groups, as well as those who primarily care about maintaining their own record of success as an advisor. This group includes advisors who exclusively support highly accomplished candidates who have the highest likelihood of being successful in their next competition. If you are not one of these top candidates, you are unlikely to get any help from this type of advisor other than their opinion that you are not ready.

Deliberate gatekeeping is not as hidden as you might think. Some university leaders argue that they play a crucial role as gatekeepers to the application process for national awards. Dr. Kyle Mox, Associate Dean for National Scholarships at Arizona State University, wrote in a 2019 op-ed that some students and faculty are too focused on the money and prestige awarded, and that these adults can "fall prey" to advising services outside the university that encourage them to apply. He claims that he and other university advisors are looking out for students' "well-being" when choosing who to provide application support. He argues, "In certain circumstances, advising a candidate not to apply for an award is the right advice, and the real success does not happen until 10 years later" (Mox 2019).

When I was in college, I was one of those students advised not to apply to a competitive fellowship because my 3.2 GPA was considered low. This discouragement only hurt my self-confidence and created an unnecessary and unfair hurdle to an application process that was already hard enough. It also angered me because I proved I was, in fact, a qualified candidate when I won the award and succeeded in the opportunity. Especially for students who face invisible challenges to achieving high grades and a stacked résumé of activities, telling some students not to apply based on a cursory review of their résumé is not just biased; it robs these students of a unique learning opportunity to work on their personal narrative and get feedback. I've never seen a candidate's well-being suffer from a mentor encouraging them to apply to a dream opportunity, even when the outcome was a rejection. Often, the encouragement proves more valuable than the award. So, if we value equal opportunity, then all interested applicants should be invited to rise to the challenge and have agency over the outcome. The award selection process can speak for itself.

The reality is, the turning away of interested students from advising happens not because the aspirants can't be successful, but because the advisor thinks they will be more difficult and time-consuming to advise, which is the deficiency of the advisor, not the candidate. Advisors and the institutions they represent are also pursuing awards and accolades that are based on the number of applicants who win, not the number of applicants they serve and advise. So the incentives for deliberate gatekeeping are high. If you are a candidate who is discouraged from applying to an opportunity because of deliberate gatekeeping, don't take this as an accurate calculation of your ability to be successful.

Well-Intentioned Gatekeeping

Even more problematic is well-intentioned gatekeeping. This comes from the protective mentor who truly cares about your well-being and wants to shield you from the pain of disappointment, unrewarded effort, discrimination, and failure. Their advice to lower your goals can stem from their own negative experiences facing rejection and discrimination or their inability to guide you on how to achieve your aspirational goal. The idea of helping candidates recalibrate their high goals to something more attainable, so that they achieve some level of success, is entrenched—and even glorified—as the correct approach in academic and career advising. It is this phenomenon that prompts students to always apply to "safety schools" and explains why women are less likely to apply for jobs where they don't meet all the job qualifications. I feel strongly that well-intentioned gatekeeping prevents millions of people from achieving their full potential. Playing it safe and avoiding disappointment is not a winning strategy for building a great career.

Throughout our popular culture, you'll find many examples of highly successful people who once received discouragement from people deemed to be experienced mentors when they expressed their big goals and sought support.

Todd Graves, the founder of Raising Cane's Chicken Fingers, a franchise restaurant company, is an example of someone who listened to his internal vision rather than external opinions. Today, Graves is a guest investor on the popular television show *Shark Tank*, where start-up companies pitch their businesses for investment. Graves explained on the show that he was once told his business ideas were not just unfeasible but bad. While an undergraduate student at Louisiana State University, his idea for Raising Cane's received the lowest grade for a start-up pitching assignment in his business class. The negative feedback did not stop there; he was rejected from many bank loans when he tried to make the business a reality. But Graves was so certain of his business vision that he saved and used more than $40,000 of his own money, plus $100,000 from friends and family and a government loan, to establish his first restaurant. The business grew, and today Raising Cane's is so successful that Graves is estimated to have a personal net worth of more than $9.5 *billion* (Wu 2024). Imagine if he had listened to the opinions of his business professors and peers when he was first starting out? Millions of business founders quit early when told their ideas are bad.

Michelle Obama is another example. She shared her childhood experiences in her book *Becoming* (Obama 2018). As a young Black woman, she had Ivy League college ambitions as I did. Her goal was entrance to Princeton University, where her older brother was studying. But when she shared her goal with her high school guidance counselor, she was discouraged. "I'm not sure that you're Princeton material," Obama remembered the counselor saying. "Her judgment was as swift as it was dismissive, probably based on some quick-glance calculus involving my grades and test scores." Obama wrote that she "deliberately and almost instantly blotted this experience out" (pp. 65–66). It turns out that erasing this experience from her mind was an effective way to cope with the negative advice that otherwise would have stopped her from pursuing her aspirational goal. Not only did Michelle Obama resolve to apply, she was selected and went on to complete her undergraduate degree at Princeton University. She later completed her juris doctorate at

Harvard Law School and built an extraordinary career as an attorney and nonprofit leader and served as First Lady of the United States. She wrote her best-selling book *Becoming* to share her challenges on the road to success and show that you don't need the external validation of others to pursue and achieve your goals. You can become what you set your sights on.

Scenes of discouragement from a trusted advisor, teacher, colleague, family member, or friend play out millions of times a day to millions of people, to the extent that it's become culturally commonplace to be told to prepare ourselves for disappointment when pursuing big goals. However, unlike Graves and Obama, most young people take this advice as "truth," not knowing the advice is often faulty and based on fear and assumptions rather than fact.

Worse, most mentors and advisors don't realize how damaging the advice to lower your goals can be for the human psyche. This discouraging advice feeds the self-doubt that people naturally grapple with and ignites the impostor syndrome that young adults carry with them well into their midlife careers. It also stops young people from experiencing ambition and failure at the level that develops a key attribute of the successful: grit. If you don't experience failure and rejection because you avoid ambitious goals, you never develop the practice of picking yourself up, improving the effort, and trying again. That resilience is necessary to achieve the highest levels of success.

If you lowered your goals based on advice from a trusted mentor, you may wonder now if that advice held you back from achieving more. It likely did, but you can change that.

Listen to Guides, Not Gatekeepers

The best mentors you can seek out are *guides*: people who have experience, insights, or expertise that are valuable to your career trajectory and who also see your potential and do not discourage you from pursuing big, aspirational goals. They see value in facing your fears and entering the competitive process, no matter what the outcome is. When you experience failure, rather than saying "I told you so," a guide will celebrate your high effort, make you feel seen, and encourage you to try again.

Lauren Wang is an example of someone who leaned into the advice of a guide rather than well-intentioned gatekeepers. She is the founder of The Flex Company. In an interview in the *Masters of Scale* podcast (Berman 2024), Wang shared that when she first had the idea to start a company that sells innovative women's period products, she didn't consider herself qualified to be a CEO, especially because she was a mid-level marketing manager and had not yet achieved the C-suite as a chief marketing officer (CMO). Some of her respected women mentors agreed. Two of them, serving as well-intentioned gatekeepers, reminded her how difficult it is to start a company and raise capital, especially as a female founder, and advised her to work at a small start-up first and experience being a CMO before taking such a big risk. At first she agreed. But Wang said her mind was changed when a male tech founder asked her to apply to be CEO of his new company. She was surprised he recognized her leadership potential. He was the guide that she needed. Wang resolved not to undertake a C-suite opportunity from others but create her own. She founded and became CEO of The Flex Co. that in 2025 grew to a successful private company with a $15 billion market cap and products in all the major chains, including Target and Walgreens.

Robyn Curtis, Director of Major Fellowships at Clemson University, is another example of a guide. Curtis was recognized for her mentorship when she was awarded the university's 2022 Frank A. Burtner Award for Excellence in Advising. During the first couple of years of Curtis's tenure as director, more than 100 Clemson students, alumni, and faculty won almost every major national award and fellowship, an outcome of her approach to advising. One of her former advisees, Daniel Custer, was accepted to a Ph.D. program in engineering at Stanford University and won a National Science Foundation fellowship; however, he wasn't immediately successful. He says Curtis mentored him on five major fellowship applications over several years, even after he graduated from Clemson. When his first round of applications was not successful, Curtis continued to advise him, fortified his self-confidence, and helped him identify projects and experiences that would make him a well-rounded candidate. Custer said of his advisor, "Robyn went above and beyond to provide kind, timely, and honest feedback to best prepare me to succeed. It was clear that helping students have the best opportunities for funding and graduate education is a priority in her life" (Cass 2022). Curtis exhibits a key attribute of guides: they won't give up on you.

Guides are rare, so when you find a mentor like this, do your best to cultivate your relationship with them. The positive emotional support they provide as you pursue big goals will help build your courage and self-confidence, which is just as important as the expertise they offer.

Distinguishing Guides from Gatekeepers

Guides are ideal mentors who provide both a high level of expertise and a high level of positive support and encouragement. *Gatekeepers* may have expertise but withhold it from some candidates; they also discourage you from pursuing high goals. As you meet potential mentors throughout your career, identify where they land on this graph of expertise and support, and cultivate relationships with guides.

(© Pitch Your Potential / Vicki Johnson, Ph.D.)

Lower Your Fear of Comparison

Beyond recognizing the mental impacts of fear of failure and messaging from gatekeepers, we also must be aware of how social media impacts the way we view ourselves and others and hurts our ability to achieve success.

One advantage I had for the growth of my self-confidence as a teenager and young adult was that I didn't have social media to remind me daily of how I compared to others. Comparison culture certainly existed through print and TV media and social experiences in my community, but without social media, it wasn't nearly as pervasive and immersive as it is now. Today, every aspect of your identity, from your physical appearance to the schools you attended to your employment status to where you live and vacation, is shared online and open to critique from friends and strangers alike. With our divisive political climate, even our very thoughts and values are a subject of comparison and comment by thousands of strangers on the Internet. Frankly, it sucks.

While there is plenty of positive social media intended to help you find your community of like-minded people, there is an equal if not greater degree of media and commercial advertising reminding you of the endless competition for limited opportunities. If you look closely at your social media feeds, you'll see attention-seeking and fear-mongering in most news, advertising, and social sharing. You'll see many "solutions" (often with a price tag) to address your fears of missing out, not fitting in, rejection, financial scarcity, and loneliness. Fear-based news about the increasing competitiveness of jobs, top universities, investments, and awards has reached a fever pitch.

Social media and the intense comparison culture it cultivates are what prompt us to share online how we have achieved our personal ambitions. More than ever, we strive to win opportunities to gain attention.

This is not to say personal ambition is bad. Every great inventor, political leader, scientist, entrepreneur, athlete, and artist has a high level of personal ambition. Ambition is the ingredient that fuels hard work, practice, consistency, and lifelong learning. I know personal ambition well; it drives me every day.

However, what we have lost collectively in the drive to fulfill our personal ambition and display "success" online is our empathy for those who hold the limited resources and opportunities we desire. We look at selection committees as feared judges rather than future collaborators and friends. We allow their selection to make a statement about our worth and a rejection to mean we're just not good enough. For the individual applicant, competition becomes about being viewed as the best, causing us to fear and compare ourselves to competitors in ways that can negatively impact our mindset.

If you weren't able to access any information about your competitors, consider how this might change your mindset about the competitions you enter for jobs, university spots, awards, and special opportunities.

Imagine that you are a young professional and aspire to achieve a promotion and move up in your career. You have discovered a conference that you would like to attend because there are sessions on the latest innovations in your field and the conference offers a chance for you to network with leaders and peers.

Consider how you would feel if you planned to make a pitch to your boss to fund your attendance to the conference. You know that your boss has discretionary funding to send you to the conference, but that funding could be used for many other things. So you create a proposal to explain why you want to go, how the conference will positively impact your work and contribution, and how you plan to leverage the opportunity for personal and professional growth after the event. You work hard on the proposal to ensure it is detailed, compelling, and beneficial to the company. You'll receive one of two answers: yes or no.

Now imagine a different scenario. Your boss announces that they will send to the conference one person from your five-person team, some of whom have been at the company longer than you. Your boss asks that each person pitch why you want to go, why you deserve the opportunity, and how it will positively impact your work and contribution. Think about how you feel now. You start to consider the attributes of your more experienced team members and what they have that you don't. You worry that the selection process won't be fair. You think about how you will look to others if you're not selected. You work hard on your proposal. You will ultimately receive one of two answers: yes or no.

Although the outcome in both scenarios is the same, a yes or no, which scenario feels more intimidating?

When this exercise is posed in my corporate trainings, the overwhelming majority always pick the latter—the group competition. The reason why is the psychology of comparison. In the first situation, there is no competitor: just you and the power of your pitch. There can be disappointment from a "No," but there is no chance of comparison with your peers because there was no competition. In the second scenario, you are concerned with how others will make their pitch and about subjective decision-making and favoritism. You worry about how losing to a competitor will look to others.

Unfortunately, many people choose not to enter competitions, or enter but sabotage their effort, solely because of the intimidation created by being compared with their peers and the fear that their failure will be exposed to others. This fear of comparison and embarrassment is why we tell people in advance of the outcome that we don't expect to be selected. We worry that others will be judgmental of our high goals and try to acknowledge the failure before it happens, to make rejection less painful and embarrassing.

But meanwhile, these very actions negatively impact our ability to succeed. By telling yourself and others that you expect to fail because of the caliber of your competitors, you train your brain to expect failure, which leads you to self-sabotage your efforts. These protective mechanisms against comparison and embarrassment cause mindset challenges like lack of confidence, procrastination, writer's block, and avoidance of constructive feedback.

Having a winner's mindset means you don't worry about what your competitors bring. You only concern yourself with being the most prepared applicant you can be, using the resources, people, knowledge, and experiences you have available to you.

Develop Your Winner's Mindset

I've never met someone who got into a highly competitive opportunity who did not sincerely believe at the deepest level that they could achieve it. A person with a winner's mindset believes they can win and that they deserve the opportunity because of the exceptionally high effort they put into their application. Even if you start with low confidence, the more intensely you prepare for a competition, the more confident you will become. Optimism and resolve are important to achieving success, which is why many professional athletes have coaches just for developing their winner's mindset.

To develop your winner's mindset, try to turn off your protective reflexes against the fears of rejection and comparison by actively changing the narrative in your mind and from your mouth. It's not arrogant to say aloud to others, "I believe I can be successful, and I'm going to apply my absolute highest effort." Do this and take note of who steps up and supports you in that effort. Those will be the same people you should turn to for support if you receive a rejection, because they will prompt you to face failure undeterred and try again.

Also, avoid making assumptions about how selectors make their decisions. Part of the reason we are so impacted by comparison culture today is that we can see who is applying for and achieving the roles, university spots, awards, and opportunities that we have our heart set on. The winners' résumés of achievement are displayed proudly online for us to analyze for clues as to why they were picked and we were rejected. Yet, from this limited information, we don't actually know the basis of the decision. We often assume it's because the winner has some things that we lack. This is true, but it's not the things you think.

It's Not a Numbers Game

Because we have limited information about how selections are made for competitive opportunities, we tend to look at people who have achieved the opportunity we desire and assume they were picked because they have better "numbers": more years of experience, more credentials, a higher GPA, more prestigious universities, more skills, more awards, better publications, or higher test scores. This creates the assumption that to win we need a better résumé. For some people, this fuels an endless drive to accrue more accolades, volunteer roles, university degrees, and certificates. Because we believe these "numbers" are the key to beating out other candidates, we also give this advice to others. When applying to Cornell back in the late 1990s, the primary advice I received was to increase my SAT score and join more extracurriculars.

Yet the competitions of our careers are never a numbers game where the winners are selected because they have the best or most achievements. No selector is numerically grading their applicants by accomplishments and choosing the person with the highest score. While it might seem that way from our limited view of the selection process—because people with big numbers often win—the primary reason certain people are selected is because they are skilled at inspiring selection committees with a compelling vision of their future potential. Those who have achieved a lot of success tend to have this skill from intergenerational knowledge shared in their family and academic networks or from experience applying to many competitive opportunities or both.

Being chosen for selective opportunities is a dynamic process of alignment and human connection. Although we don't start on a level playing field when it comes to access to quality education and intergenerational knowledge, everyone can learn the skills to communicate a story of the future, leveraging their unique lived experience, to inspire a selection committee and become a standout candidate.

Likewise, the reason people with impressive résumés don't always win is because they were up against a competitor who was more prepared and provided a more compelling vision of their future potential. In any competition, a record of achievement cannot compensate for a lack of one of the most important ingredients for success: authentic desire.

The Advantage of Authentic Desire

Whenever someone asks me if applying to a highly competitive opportunity is worth the effort, I know that they don't yet have a defined purpose and authentic desire for the opportunity. They are more concerned about the effort than the extraordinary things that could be gained from the opportunity and the pursuit.

This realization is not necessarily a bad thing. You should not waste time applying to opportunities that you don't have a clear need for. In any competition, you will be up against a small subset of candidates who are driven by purpose and who authentically desire the opportunity. Even if they have not yet learned how to apply all the strategies necessary to get picked by a selection committee, they will be top contenders because of their enthusiasm and will reap rewards from the application process, including new knowledge, practice, and relationships that will only benefit them in the future. Rather than feel dejected, a rejection will embolden this group to try harder and try again. That resilient mindset is created from authentic desire.

One challenge is that many of us don't know why we should want a particular opportunity beyond the fact that it might make us look successful to others. Often, our career goals are developed through the lens of our family's definition of success. Some young people feel pressure to pursue careers in medicine, law, the military, the family business, or academia because the career track means to the family that you've achieved morality, prestige, security, or wealth.

However, if your career pursuits are not aligned with your authentic desires, one of two things will happen: either you will quit before you achieve the goal because the effort is both difficult and unrewarding, or you will achieve the career goal but become frustrated and disillusioned with the work. This disillusionment with a career track often happens between ages 35 and 45, also known as the infamous "midlife crisis."

To avoid this, it's important for you to intentionally explore and decide what your personal mission will be for the near future so that you can pursue opportunities that are personally fulfilling. This exploration also helps you find new, exciting opportunities you couldn't have imagined or planned for earlier in your career that perfectly align with your deepest interests and dreams for your life. The excitement to achieve those opportunities is *authentic desire*.

When you apply to an opportunity that you authentically desire, you will automatically have an advantage over candidates who are applying for superficial reasons. Authentic desire produces the energy and focus you need to go above and beyond and become the most prepared applicant in the competition.

The strategies in this book are going to help you to find your purpose—your personal mission—so that you can find, recognize, and competitively apply to exceptional opportunities that you truly desire and bypass those you don't.

With the winner's mindset, intentionality, and authentic desire, you have the mental fortitude to be a top competitor in any competitive sphere you enter. The next step is refining your approach to the competition.

Writing a Compelling Personal Pitch

Most of the competitions of our career start with writing. We apply for jobs by preparing a cover letter and résumé. We apply for college and graduate school by preparing a personal statement. We request resources for a promotion or special project by writing a proposal. We enter business accelerators and investment negotiations by preparing a pitch deck. Although our pursuit of these opportunities might start with a conversation or connection, we can't be fairly considered among other candidates without something written about who we are and what our goals are.

While it is an advantage to be a good writer, not all experienced writers have mastered the art of writing a persuasive pitch that effectively answers the question "Why you?" People who have mastered creative, journalistic, and academic writing often struggle the most to prepare a compelling personal pitch.

Now, generative artificial intelligence (AI) writing tools may help level the playing field by enabling everyone to create a functional personal pitch. But what happens when we reach the stage where virtually everyone is using AI tools to apply for competitive opportunities? Even if fundamentally we are all more coherent in our communications, most candidates' applications will sound the same, just as they do today.

Meanwhile, a small number of people will hone and leverage their own human creativity and originality to stand out. I want you to be one of those people.

Persuasive communication skills, which are built from the tenets of great storytelling, are the key to building an exciting career and becoming an exceptional competitor. Like all great stories, the story that you tell to answer the question "Why you?" must have a clear beginning, a middle, and an end, with a "hook" that captures what you need to get from where you are now to where you want to be in the future. Once you learn how to tell a persuasive story in writing, you'll find that this skill also helps you become a persuasive speaker who can nail interviews, negotiations, and spot conversations that lead to investment.

Your story is a lot more than just finding the right words; it's about finding the angle that will make a personal connection with the selectors. Your pitch must be highly aligned with the pitch selectors make to their stakeholders on how they approach the problems they aim to solve.

Your Winning Application Story

When I talk about your story in the course of this book, I'm not talking about the story of your life, although that is part of it. Rather, I'm talking about your *application story*, the response to the question "Why you?" that you need to provide whenever you are in a competition for a cherished opportunity.

Every application story has a beginning, a middle, and an end. Often, you will discuss the beginning and end of the story first in your written applications and interviews. The middle "hook" is the most critical piece of the application story, often discussed last in your pitch for emphasis.

The *beginning* of the story is your background up until this point, supported with memorable anecdotes that explain the motivations behind your career choices and who you are as a person.

The *end* of the story is in the future, after the opportunity you are striving for. The end is the achievement of your highly specific and timely goal, which has a positive impact on others that fulfills both your ambition and personal mission and fulfills the organization's mission, making your selection mutually beneficial. This part of the story defines your future potential.

The *middle*, the story *hook*, is where you couch the organization as the "hero" needed to achieve the goal. You express how the organization offers unique benefits that you will capitalize on to achieve your future goal while advancing the organization's mission. Without the organization's unique benefits, the goal may not be achieved.

The Winning Application Story

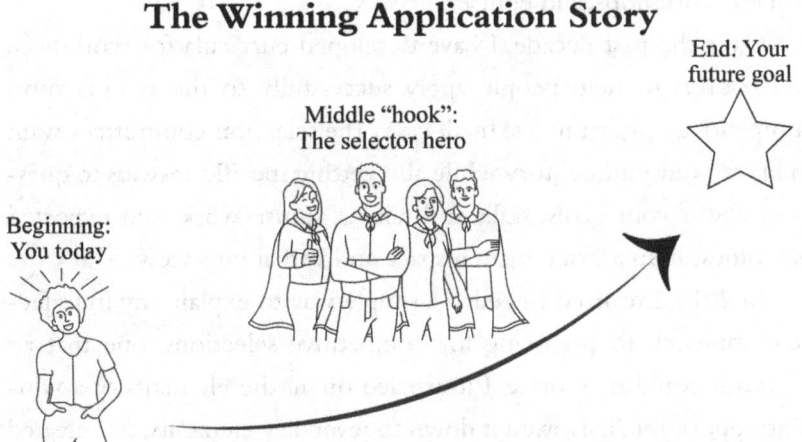

The winning application story is a story outline that helps you present a clear, compelling expression of why you should be selected. The beginning of the story is your background and motivations for your career choices. The end of the story is the achievement of your highly specific goal that has a positive impact on others. The middle "hook" is how the selectors' opportunity offers unique benefits that you will capitalize on to achieve your future goal and further their mission.

(© Pitch Your Potential / Vicki Johnson, Ph.D.)

The MATCH ME Formula®

The MATCH ME Formula® is a tested, tactical approach to developing an exceptional application story that wins you opportunities that have a competitive application process.

In 2011, my husband Ryan and I founded ProFellow®, an organization that helps level the playing field for competitive educational and professional opportunities by making information about fellowships, graduate study, awards, and accelerators more publicly accessible. At ProFellow.com, we advance our mission by providing a free, searchable database of thousands of competitive opportunities for people at all career levels, as well as application advice through high-quality articles, workshops, and courses.

Over the past decade, I have developed curricula for workshops and courses to help people apply successfully to the world's most competitive opportunities. In all cases, the selection committees want to know your unique story while also getting specific answers to questions about your goals, skills and talents, future work, and expected outcomes, all in a brief written space and verbal interview.

In 2019, I realized I needed a simple way to explain my multifaceted approach to preparing for competitive selections, one that an applicant could memorize. I journaled on all the elements of a winning application, narrowed it down to seven key elements, and created an acronym for it: the MATCH ME Formula®.

The MATCH ME Formula® is a strategic approach to answer the question "Why you?" and effectively communicate your unique skills, background, and career goals to stand out in any competition. The secret sauce of the MATCH ME Formula® is the incorporation of alignment and reciprocity.

Not only does the MATCH ME Formula® encompass seven individual elements, but the two words *Match Me* also represent the power of matching your personal mission with the organizational mission of groups that provide special opportunities and resources.

> **The MATCH ME Formula®**
>
> M = Memorable
> A = Aligns with the organization's mission
> T = Timely
> C = Capitalizes on the organization's unique benefits
> H = Highly specific
> M = Mutually beneficial
> E = Elegant
>
> **Each letter of MATCH ME represents an element of a winning application. When applied to a competitive job, university, or award application, these seven elements help your application stand out as exceptional.**
>
> (© Pitch Your Potential / Vicki Johnson, Ph.D.)

This book will teach you how to interpret and apply the MATCH ME Formula®, with supporting research and case studies of ordinary people who have applied the formula to break through periods of self-doubt, comparison, and rejection to achieve their most aspirational goals. Namely, this formula will guide your approach to:

- Land dream jobs
- Get accepted to top universities
- Win fellowships and other prestigious awards
- Negotiate promotions or resources for special projects
- Win business pitch competitions and attract investors
- Land special opportunities like speaking engagements and board positions
- Build a large professional network that will increasingly fuel your career growth

You don't need a high degree of self-confidence to begin applying these strategies for success. The beauty of the MATCH ME Formula® is that as you work to apply the seven formulaic elements, you will gain greater confidence in your pitch and ability to answer the pressing question "Why you?" The formula is like a fitness regimen to prepare for competitive opportunities that will help you unlock what you are truly capable of. When you put in your highest effort, you will feel more confident that you don't just want—but truly *deserve*—the achievement of extraordinary opportunities that are aligned with your values, deepest desires, and personal mission for social impact.

Key Takeaways

- Fear of failure is a positive signal that you have found an opportunity that you have an authentic desire to achieve. Lean in emotionally to the possibility of success to put in your absolute highest effort.
- Deliberate and well-intentioned gatekeepers will give you advice to lower your goals. Career and academic advice are opinions, not facts, so resolve to aim for high goals despite discouraging advice.
- Cultivate relationships with guides: people who have useful expertise and knowledge and who also positively support you in pursuing your highest goals.
- We make the wrong assumptions about the criteria for selection, so don't concern yourself with the résumés of your competitors. Focus solely on the unique experiences, skills, and ideas you have to offer and developing a compelling vision of your future potential.
- Do not be ashamed of failure and rejection. If you put in your highest effort, others will notice you in the best possible way, which will result in future opportunities that you cannot imagine now.

- Your *application story* is the response to the selectors' question "Why you?" It includes a beginning (your background and motivations), a middle "hook" (how you will capitalize on their unique benefits to achieve a mutually beneficial outcome), and an end (your future goal).
- The MATCH ME Formula® is a tested, tactical approach to developing an exceptional application story that wins you opportunities that have a competitive application process.

How to Use This Book

To make the most of the "Your Turn" exercises at the end of each chapter on the seven elements of the MATCH ME Formula®, choose one dream opportunity that you will use for the exercises. That could be your dream job, a top graduate program, a fellowship or award, a business accelerator, a leadership role like a board position, or any other opportunity that has a competitive application process and many other contenders.

2 | Become Memorable

Stick in the Minds of the Selection Committee

In the fall of 2024, I was sitting in a conference room with more than 100 executive-level women from HiPower, where *Sail to Scale* author Mona Sabet was presenting on how women can build influence to achieve their professional goals. My ears perked up when she began to speak on tactics to stand out and become memorable when introducing yourself or making a cold pitch by email to potential investors.

With the big presentation screen glowing behind her, Mona clicked to a slide with a picture of a smiling young man, John (not his real name), who was an early employee of an overseas tech start-up. In the picture, John is standing on the rooftop of a city skyscraper, holding up two to-go cups of coffee to the camera. One cup had a hand-scrawled name, "John," and the other, "Mona."

Mona said, "John reached out to me by email, with this picture attached, to make a sales pitch for his start-up's product."

"I get so many cold emails," she continued. "I rarely respond to salespeople. So likewise, I didn't respond to John's initial email. But this picture he attached made me smile, and it definitely got my attention."

"A few days later," Mona went on, "John sent me a follow-up email with another picture."

She clicked to the next slide. It was a picture of John on the same rooftop, now holding up two cold bottles of Corona, complete with a slice of lime squeezed in the open bottle necks.

"He wrote, 'Maybe you're not a coffee drinker . . . so how about a beer on me?'" Mona smirked, and the room erupted in laughter.

Mona explained that although she receives and passes over hundreds of sales pitch emails, she noticed John's outreach and selectively chose to respond to him, not because he had an extraordinary product but because he was creative in getting her attention in a positive way. His approach was memorable.

Even more interesting to me, John's approach was so memorable that years later, Mona now uses this encounter as a case study on how to become more effective in self-introductions. Probably unbeknownst to John at the time of Mona's presentation, John's memorable pitch created a positive, long-term ripple effect of influence.

Mona and John's story exemplifies the first letter M in the MATCH ME Formula®, which stands for *Memorable*. **The key to being memorable is to create "stickiness" that will last in the minds of the selectors long after they have been introduced to you in person or in writing.** In all cases, you want to make a positive impression, not a negative one.

In this chapter, you will learn:

- Why being memorable matters
- Five factors of positive memorability
- Four ways to "stick" in the selector's mind

Why Being Memorable Matters

It's simple to understand why being memorable in a positive way matters: if your written application, email request, proposal, or interview is so vague or bland that it is quickly forgotten among the many others, or is memorable in a negative way, you've abandoned your shot at getting considered for selection. To get noticed, you want to make it easier for selectors to notice you and give you further consideration, especially for dream opportunities.

More and more people are entering the global competition for jobs, university spots, awards, and investment, creating a lot of noise from the tens to thousands of people who are seeking the selectors' attention. The exponential increase in applicants over the past several years was fueled first by the advent of online job platforms that offer "one-click" application features and more recently by the release of generative AI tools like ChatGPT that enable a lot more people to create and send a cover letter or application quickly. *Time* magazine reported (Semuels 2023) that within the job market since 2023, there is, on average, one job opening for every two applicants on LinkedIn.com, up from early 2022, when there was on average one job opening per applicant. Today, jobs at the corporate level now receive on average 250 applicants (Glassdoor Team 2015), with some big-name companies on the far end of the spectrum, like Google, which annually receives two million job applications for just 4,000 positions, a 0.2% "acceptance" rate (Quantic 2022).

This phenomenon is also reflected in the increasing number of college and graduate school applications. The Council of Graduate Schools found that post-pandemic, U.S. graduate schools that exclusively offer master's degrees experienced a more than 18% increase in applications, and top doctoral programs had 10% more applicants than in previous years (Knox 2023). At Harvard College alone, the acceptance rate for the undergraduate freshman classes has declined from about 10.5% in 2003 to 3.2% in 2023 (Schisgall and Shah 2023), reflecting an increase in applicants with no increase in spots. A large portion of new U.S. university applicants are from foreign countries, making the competition truly global.

While new tools are enabling more applications, they are not necessarily creating better candidates. I suspect that the majority of candidates today still lack a memorable angle in their written job, school, and award applications because they are preparing applications quickly and passively, with an overreliance on AI tools for writing and tailoring. That's not a great strategy to get noticed. Stats show that 80% of employers in 2024 dislike AI-generated résumés and cover letters (Robinson 2024). These tech innovations are creating more poor-quality applications for hiring managers to sift through, not necessarily more high-caliber candidates for you to contend with—at least for now.

It's arguable that AI tools will get better and better in helping you create a good application for selective opportunities, but even then, all AI improvements will really do is raise the bar of expectations of what is considered a strong application worthy of closer attention. Your application still needs an element of originality to garner attention. Using a tool that makes everyone sound better, but the same, won't help you.

I also suspect that once the sheer number of applications becomes unmanageable for organizations (and some may have already reached this stage), a greater portion of opportunities will be taken offline and shared only through referrals and trusted networks. This is another reason why it's so important to be a memorable candidate throughout your career.

I have spent a lot of time experimenting with ways to make myself memorable to the members of selection committees and have found that there are five factors of positive memorability that help you build relationships with selectors and create applications that they remember long after reading.

Five Factors of Positive Memorability

When we introduce ourselves in a memorable way or create a written application that is memorable, we are telling a story about our past and future selves. We use stories to share who we are and what influences our career path, we use stories to express new ideas, and we share stories about our relationships when someone makes an introduction on our behalf.

As you communicate with selectors and tell stories, five factors of positive memorability will help make you and your story "sticky"—positively remembered in the mind of the receivers long after they have been introduced to you in person or in writing. A story or experience that is memorable is:

1. **Detailed:** Visual and tactile detail helps the selector understand, notice, and retell the personal anecdote, idea, or mutual relationship you share. If expressing an idea for the future, use as much detail as possible so the person can imagine the physical outcome of this idea in their mind.

2. **Novel:** The mutual contact, anecdote, or idea has a high likelihood of being different than that of other candidates.

3. **Meaningful:** The mutual relationship, personal anecdote, or idea demonstrates that you embody the characteristics of the selector's ideal candidate without saying it directly, creating underlying meaning. Your ideas and relationships can help exhibit your resourcefulness, leadership or service experience,

passion for a subject, creativity, commitment, and intellectual curiosity, among others.

4. **Personal:** When sharing stories about your lived experience, you may have incredible stories to share that feature the feats of your parents, friends, or people you have helped. However, stories that feature other people do not provide the selectors with useful information about you. If, for example, you want to talk about how your parents' experience influenced you and your career path, keep your personal anecdote focused on your metamorphosis from their influence, not the details of your parents' lives.

5. **Positive:** Use personal anecdotes and ideas that are primarily positive. While shocking stories can indeed make you memorable, you may be remembered in a negative way. When discussing a personal challenge from your lived experience, use your limited space to emphasize the positive outcomes and transformation you experienced, rather than the details of the challenge.

To apply these factors to become more memorable, as a first step, you must consider where you have opportunities to create "stickiness," either in person or in writing.

At the beginning of this chapter, I shared John's unique way of introducing himself to Mona. His approach was memorable and stood out because it was novel, had visual detail in his photos of the coffee cups and Coronas, and was positive because it was funny!

As great as John's approach was, it likely will be challenging for you to come up with such an original, quirky idea. I don't recommend heading up to your rooftop with two cups of coffee and a Sharpie to snap a pic like John's to send to someone on a selection committee. Copycat ideas typically don't have the same effect as the original. If you have the imagination to come up with an original way to introduce yourself or garner attention and you feel confident that it would leave a positive impression (not a negative one), I say, try it! It's great practice to try small experiments like these throughout your career to help you build confidence in your ideas and figure out what works and what doesn't.

For the majority of us who feel less imaginative or are pressured by the time crunch to come up with a way to be memorable, there are four simpler strategies I recommend. In their order of effectiveness, they are:

1. Getting a referral to selectors through a mutual contact
2. Making a self-introduction and engaging in a conversation using "double whammy" questions
3. Pitching a memorable idea that is novel and has high detail
4. Incorporating a memorable anecdote about you from your lived experience

Get a Referral from a Mutual Contact

An introduction to a selector from a mutual contact in your network, also known as a *referral*, is a powerful way to garner attention and be memorable. Your "network" is simply everyone you know from your personal life and community, your academic studies, your jobs, and other experiences like travel, activity groups, and events. People often assume they are not connected to anyone who can give them a referral, but this is hard to know unless you keep digital documentation of who is in your network and can see your contacts' networks through a digital platform like LinkedIn (see Tip).

A direct referral, ideally with a positive note about your background and skills, demonstrates to the selector that you are part of a trusted network and are likely to have the qualities the selector is looking for. It provides external validation from someone they trust. The more influential the mutual contact is, the more powerful and memorable the referral will be. Referrals take different forms depending on what you are applying for:

- **When applying for a job or internship,** a referral can come from people who work inside the organization or through an organization's board member, advisor, or former employee.
- **For graduate programs,** a referral can come from faculty and administrators who personally know those on the selection committee or from a current student or alumnus.
- **For awards and fellowships,** a referral can come from a previous winner (and often award programs leverage their alumni network for nominations).
- **For investors and business accelerators,** a referral can come from a mutual contact who knows the investors or program staff.

To secure a referral to selectors for an opportunity you desire, a person from your network can:

- Introduce you to a selector they know personally by email or in person
- Write a recommendation letter or provide their contact information as a reference
- Put in a good word for you without making an introduction (more common in formal application processes)

Follow these steps to receive effective referrals that help you land introductions, receive a positive response, and build your network in the process:

1. **When asking someone for an introduction to a selector, provide them with a blurb for the introduction so you can have some control over the message.** Ideally, the

introduction includes an explanation of who you are and why you are seeking an introduction. It is even better if your introduction includes a glowing reference to your talents or accomplishments.
2. **Be prepared to respond swiftly once you are introduced to a selector.** As the candidate being introduced, you should respond to the introduction immediately, within 24 hours (otherwise, your referring colleague may never make a referral again!). Then give the person you were introduced to three business days to respond to your email before following up.
3. **Once connected, be prepared with specific questions that can't be answered from their website or are too broad to answer simply.** If you ask the selector a broad or vague question, like "How do I get a job at your company?," this can make a bad impression, the opposite of your goal. A specific question that can be answered simply can be something like "What specific technical skills are the Communications team looking for in candidates?"

You should demonstrate that you have done your research about the person and the opportunity before speaking with them and use focused questions that will draw out useful information that is not found online.

Example: Requesting a Referral After I planned and executed a full-day Women in Leadership Symposium for the Einhorn Center at Cornell University, I asked the center's director, Basil Safi, who gave me positive feedback on the event, if he could introduce me to other departments at Cornell that may be offering speaking opportunities. In particular, I was interested in being introduced to a leader at Cornell's Tatcon Center for New Students.

After I provided Basil with some language to include, here is what he wrote to introduce me to the director of the Tatkon Center:

By way of email, it's my pleasure to introduce you to Vicki Johnson, a class of '01 alum who's been deeply involved with the Einhorn Center over the past several years. Vicki is looking to ramp up her connections to campus and is particularly drawn to the work of the Tatkon Center. She's particularly interested in any speaking or programming opportunities with new student orientation. She facilitated an event for us in NYC last summer and was absolutely terrific. I hope you two have an opportunity to speak at some point soon.

This introduction effectively got the director's attention, and he immediately responded, which led to a new professional connection and opportunities.

If I had introduced myself, the response may have come, but it might not have been so immediate or receptive. An introduction from an influential mutual contact is the most effective way of making a memorable connection with a selector because someone they know and respect is vouching for you.

 **Tip: Use LinkedIn to keep digital documentation of your network for mutual and self-introductions.**

A powerful and easy platform for building and viewing digital documentation of your network is LinkedIn.com. Through LinkedIn, you can create a personal profile, like a digital résumé, and connect directly with everyone you know and meet through your universities, jobs, groups, events, family, and friendships.

The power of having a network of contacts on LinkedIn is that you can view your contacts' networks. Unless you use a tool like LinkedIn, you may never know your college roommate's uncle is the CEO of the company you want to work for or that

> a former colleague from your first job is on the board of an organization you want to be part of.
>
> Use LinkedIn to build and maintain access to your network and identify who can give you introductions to selectors that you are not directly connected to. Keep your profile updated so that you can also make self-introductions to selectors and people with whom you have common interests, like alumni from your alma mater, people in your field of work with a similar job title, and members of your local community, among others.
>
> © Pitch Your Potential / Vicki Johnson, Ph.D.

Make a Self-Introduction to a Selector

Even if you don't have a mutual contact to introduce you to a selector, you should consider making a self-introduction to stand out among the competition, ideally in person. Whenever possible, place yourself where selectors will be so you can introduce yourself, ask thoughtful questions, and create a memorable connection before submitting a digital application.

It's becoming a lot less common for students and professionals to engage in the "old-school" methods of in-person engagement with selectors, like visiting a campus, attending a career fair, calling an organization, or stopping by a company's office to drop off a physical copy of your résumé (yes, we used to do that!). *Inside Higher Education* reported that even when campuses opened in 2022, after the pandemic subsided, many students were still not attending in-person events like career fairs, workshops, social gatherings, conferences, and even sports events (Mowreader 2024). Anecdotally, I heard from college and university administrators at institutions of all types that they struggled to get students to show up for in-person events, including ones that would introduce them to future employers. Although attendance is creeping back up in 2025, universities report that it's still nowhere near the levels of attendance at in-person events pre-pandemic.

This phenomenon is something that every applicant should take advantage of now. Being one of the few who show up and make connections at in-person events of all kinds can help you build relationships with future employers, admissions representatives, investors, and award selectors, as well as peers and leaders who can refer you to new opportunities. There is even scientific evidence to support the value of physically getting your name and face in front of selectors before you apply.

When I was younger, I wondered why local elections prompted candidates to post signs all over town with just their name in bold letters but little else. Usually, these signs tell you nothing more than that someone named SHIVANI PATEL is running for an office. Unless we have seen them on TV or paper fliers, we don't even know what the candidates look like, let alone their opinions on issues. Yet, because of this signage, we see the candidate's name 10, 20, or sometimes more than a 100 times before Election Day.

There is a psychological explanation for the use and influence of name-based election signs like these, backed by research. The "Ben Griffen experiment" was one such research study, conducted in 2011 by Vanderbilt professors Dr. Cindy Kam and Dr. Elizabeth Zechmeister. During the study, the name of a fake candidate, "Ben Griffin," was put on election signs and posted in a heavily trafficked spot in Nashville, Tennessee, to see if name recognition alone had any influence on voter preferences.

The study found that among people who had driven by the signs, more than 20% of respondents to a voter preference survey chose "Ben Griffin" among their top three candidates for an at-large council seat, despite knowing nothing about him except his name. The results were found to be significant when compared to the survey results of a control group who did not drive in the same area.

Based on similar results from additional experiments, Kam and Zechmeister concluded that people tend to favor candidates with more familiar names and even consider them more viable. Consequently, manufacturing name recognition through signs and other advertising is a strategy that many election candidates use to increase their chances of success.

You can leverage this psychological phenomenon to increase your chances of success in a competition that has many contenders. You can help the selectors remember you and think of you favorably by meeting them in person before they receive your written application or pitch.

The following are some ways you can become memorable by engaging physically before the selection process begins:

1. **Attend opportunities to meet and speak with selectors in person and online.** Go to program information sessions, campus tours, conferences, business pitch events, industry events, and career and graduate school fairs. Many events are now virtual, but if an in-person option is available, take it whenever possible. Be prepared to introduce yourself and initiate a conversation with questions.
2. **Give out a business card with your headshot.** Thanks to online networking platforms like LinkedIn, physical business cards are becoming increasingly uncommon, making them a distinct advantage for you. If you are attending in-person events where selection committee members will be, bring a stack of business cards that include your professional headshot, your full name in big bold font, your email address, and a brief headline, whether that is your current job title or something related to what you do or who you want to be, such as "Aspiring Scholar in Political Science" or "Building AI Models to Address Climate Change."
3. **Connect with people you meet in person on LinkedIn with a note.** Even if you are handing out business cards when meeting in person, don't forget to connect with them on LinkedIn to create a long-term digital connection. Always add a note to your connection request to remind them how and where you met. Make sure your LinkedIn profile is up-to-date and includes a professional headshot so you can help them place your face with your name.

If you can't meet selectors in person, the next option is to introduce yourself by email. Emails are easily left unread or ignored and sometimes go to a Spam folder without our knowledge, but you might have the best success reaching out to a selector for a self-introduction through LinkedIn messaging.

Whether you introduced yourself through an in-person or online meeting or through an email, it's important that you are prepared with specific questions to make the engagement meaningful and memorable to the selector. If you are strategic with the questions you choose to ask, you can boost your name's "stickiness" in the mind of the selector.

"Double Whammy" Questions When you are meeting selectors, try to engage them for at least 5–10 minutes so they have a greater frame of reference of who you are when they see your name on a future application. If you are at a busy event, you might not have much time to engage. So your goal is to politely introduce yourself and ask two to three "double whammy" questions.

A "double whammy" question to a selector or someone of influence will do two things:

1. It will allow you to gather important information about the opportunity that you might not be able to find online, giving you an advantage over other candidates.
2. It will help demonstrate that you are thinking strategically about how you would excel in the opportunity if selected.

I provide some question examples that meet these two criteria (see the "Examples of 'Double Whammy' Questions for Conversations with Selectors" box). Be sure to choose or modify questions that make sense for the opportunity you are discussing with the selectors, whether it is a job, graduate school spot, fellowship or award, business investment, board position, or other competitive opportunity.

Examples of "Double Whammy" Questions for Conversations with Selectors

- What have been some of the most exciting or impactful outcomes of people in this program/role?
- What are some of the key strategic initiatives that the organization is addressing in the next 12 months?
- What types of people excel in this organization/role/program?
- What project/research topics would you like to see from applicants in the future that address a priority or fill a gap?
- Does the organization have any partnerships that someone in this position could leverage to help their project or work succeed?
- How is success measured in this program/role?
- What is an example of an impactful project that a person in this role has executed recently? What were the key outcomes?
- What kinds of mentorship/collaboration opportunities/alumni engagement opportunities exist in this role/program?
- What is something about being part of this program/initiative/team that people only learn once they begin?
- What are the biggest challenges the organization is facing in the next 12 months that this role would help address?

A "double whammy" question to a selector (1) allows you to gather important information about the opportunity that you might not be able to find online, giving you an advantage, and (2) helps you demonstrate that you are thinking strategically about how you would excel in the opportunity if selected.

(© Pitch Your Potential / Vicki Johnson, Ph.D.)

Any time you are able to introduce yourself and engage in a conversation with a selector or someone of influence, document the name and title of the person you met and their responses right after your conversation so you can refer to them again.

Whenever possible, write a follow-up thank-you email to the person you met, or request a LinkedIn connection and a note, and mention something you discussed. This will help them remember you in the future when you submit an application, proposal, or pitch.

Just keep in mind, attempts to get your name and face in front of selectors, or to introduce yourself by email, can quickly become unfavorable if you act in a way that seems pushy, self-centered, or ingratiating. Always take advantage of the opportunities that selectors offer to meet them and ask questions, rather than pass up these events to make a different type of connection. When meeting with selectors and influential people online or in person, be professional in your appearance and how you speak and act, and follow cultural rules of etiquette.

Propose a Memorable Idea

Proposing a memorable idea in your written application, proposal, or pitch helps you get noticed and ultimately selected. The idea could be your project or research proposal for funding, your idea to help the organization achieve its goals if you are selected for the job, or a pitch deck for a new company seeking investment or partners.

To make your idea more memorable, apply the five factors of memorability. To reiterate, your idea should be (1) detailed, (2) novel, (3) meaningful, (4) personal, and (5) positive.

Coming up with creative and memorable ideas to add to an application is a skill that comes from the ongoing practice of writing and incorporating ideas from different areas of your life: personal, academic, and professional. There is no right or wrong way to develop novel ideas, but by following the five factors of memorability in the presentation of your ideas, you'll increase your chances of being positively remembered.

To become more creative in developing new ideas, keep a diary of philosophies, frameworks, interesting research, quotes, artists, and historical events that you find yourself turning to over and over again. As you become more experienced in preparing pitches for aspirational opportunities, you'll find yourself drawing on seemingly disparate ideas and expertise gained from your personal experiences to create an idea that is novel and unlikely to be proposed by another contender.

Example: Creating a Memorable Essay Idea I've known travel writer Sojourner White (thesojournies.com) for several years and have had the pleasure of watching her pursue a unique career adventure. As a young professional social worker in 2020, Sojourner was suddenly forced to work online with her clients when the pandemic hit, so she became a remote social worker. Creatively, she took this opportunity to pursue a personal passion: travel. She began to post stories about her travel experiences on Instagram and before long, garnered a huge following, especially among Black women travelers like her who were inspired by her videos and helpful tips. Today, she is a full-time entrepreneur and has turned her passion for travel into a career in content creation and travel marketing. She was able to pursue this path successfully because she had developed a wide range of communications skills, as well as self-confidence, in her early career as she experimented with a variety of pursuits.

Sojourner's journey to becoming a successful travel writer began during her junior year in college at Bradley University, when a professor encouraged her to apply for a prestigious post-graduate Fulbright award to Spain. She had doubts she could win this award. The Fulbright U.S. Student Award program is one of the most well-known and competitive international fellowship programs in the world. Its primary mission is to strengthen the relationship between the United

States and other countries by sending abroad Americans who will make American culture and people more visible and positively viewed, and who will also bring cultural learning experiences back home. Each year, the program receives thousands of applications from American college seniors and young professionals. In recent years, Spain was the most popular country for the Fulbright English Teaching Assistantship (ETA) Award that Sojourner would apply to, receiving on average 800 applications for about 175 spots, a 22% acceptance rate.

Sojourner's professors saw that she was a great fit for the Fulbright ETA award because she was a dual Spanish and psychology major, had experience studying abroad in Spain, and had relevant experience volunteering in English language classrooms. But Fulbright receives applications from many high-caliber candidates from top schools who have a background like Sojourner's, so there was still a need for her to find an angle to stand out.

In researching the Fulbright awards, Sojourner noticed that in the 2015–2016 award year, Black candidates made up only 5% of the 1,900 Fulbright grantees (Kueppers 2016). Historically, Black American college students have faced challenges to studying abroad, including financial barriers, lack of support from family, racism, and insufficient outreach and mentoring in the process (Parker 2022). Sojourner knew that if she won the Fulbright award, she could be a model of the benefits of studying abroad for future generations of Black candidates.

This inspired her unique idea to use the seven principles of Kwanzaa to describe her identity and values in her Fulbright personal statement and show how she would share African American culture abroad. Kwanzaa is a weeklong cultural holiday in December where African American families and communities come together to honor their ancestors and celebrate their culture. The Kwanzaa principles are Umoja (unity), Kujichagulia (self-determination), Ujima (collective work and responsibility), Ujamaa (cooperative economics), Nia (purpose), Kuumba (creativity), and Imani (faith). She used these principles as a framework to describe choices she made in the past, which emphasized her interest in learning about other cultures, and her future career goals, which centered on contributing to education and public service. This approach to her personal statement made it a compelling application story that demonstrated why she was an excellent fit for a Fulbright award.

After several months of waiting for the response (a period she laughingly called "terrifying"), she screamed when she received her Fulbright acceptance letter. When I asked what she believed made her application stand out, she said, "I'm confident that I was the only applicant who used the Kwanzaa principles in their Fulbright statement." I agreed. The idea was novel, detailed, positive, and meaningful, expressing how she embodied the characteristics of their ideal candidate.

Use Memorable Anecdotes from Your Life

A final approach that anyone can use to become memorable is incorporating a personal anecdote (an old or recent memory) using vivid detail into your written application. Effective personal anecdotes will trigger both the emotional and rational receptors of your audience's brains, making them "sticky" in the mind of the recipient.

To be effective, the anecdote from your life should include enough detail for the recipient to be able to retell your story to someone else. Therefore, choose words that help the reader visualize you and the scene in their mind, including your approximate age, the physical space where the experience happened, and the emotions you were feeling at the time.

The anecdote should also demonstrate, rather than tell, the type of person you are. Through a story, you can show the things that have motivated your choice of career, your passions, and your positive impact on others without saying it directly, making it meaningful. For example, if you give an anecdote about your experience teaching a math lesson to first-grade children using a new learning method you developed, you indirectly express that you care about children and their education and that you have ingenuity and drive.

When choosing anecdotes to share, be careful not to use ones that will invoke sadness, anger, or pity in the recipient, such as a detailed story about experiencing poverty, abuse, or significant health challenges. Although a shock or trauma story could indeed be memorable and attention-grabbing, using negative anecdotes may make the recipient uncomfortable and generate negative feelings that will be unconsciously associated with your application. Anecdotes can also raise unanswered questions about your emotional and physical readiness for the competitive opportunity you are pursuing. While a personal challenge can be mentioned, detail the positive outcomes and transformation you experienced, not the challenge itself.

Example: Incorporating a Memorable Anecdote in a Personal Statement I worked with Julie Gardella, who had a unique career path before entering graduate school. After college, she spent two years in Alaska serving communities by supporting local initiatives for small businesses and entrepreneurship. When she was ready to apply to graduate school, it was important to her to receive funding, so she targeted top graduate schools that offered funding and national graduate fellowships that were highly competitive. She worked hard and was accepted to several top graduate schools, including New York University's Master in Environmental Health Sciences with full funding through a Graduate Assistantship, and the University of Massachusetts–Amherst's Master in Business Administration (MBA), which offered her a full-tuition Isenberg Fellowship.

In her successful MBA personal statement, Julie incorporated a memorable anecdote that expressed her entrepreneurial drive without saying it directly. She wrote:

> I earned my very first dollar picking up pinecones. In my grandfather's front yard grew an enormous pine tree, with long branches that stretched over the grass. My mother offered to pay one penny for every pinecone we picked up, thinking this would be a clever way to clear up the lawn and teach us about the value of earning our money. She figured our short attention spans would amount to just a few pinecones each and that she

could probably cover payroll with the spare change in her purse. She was absolutely right about my brother and cousins, who lasted about twenty minutes before they cashed in and ran off to play. Not me. I stayed out there filling bag after bag with pinecones, almost convincing myself that each one was an actual penny. I filled four huge garbage bags of pinecones before I was tired enough to call it quits. When my mom saw how many pinecones I had collected, her eyes widened and her jaw dropped; she could not believe how many I had gathered. She counted out four one-dollar bills and handed them to me. Four dollars felt like a lot of purchasing power to an eight-year-old in the early 2000s.

This anecdote meets the five factors of positive memorability, which contributed to her successful application. The anecdote uses vivid detail, allowing the reader to see the scene in their own mind; has underlying meaning about her entrepreneurial skills and drive, demonstrating she has the characteristics of their ideal candidate; is primarily about Julie; is positive and has emotional impact; and is novel. It's unlikely any competitor shared this same personal story.

This anecdote also does an excellent job of laying the foundation for the next phase in her essay (shared in full in Chapter 9), where she explains her career trajectory into business and her motivation for pursuing an MBA. Her full essay painted the picture that she is highly aligned with the school's training mission and that she has high potential for success.

Memorable anecdotes can also be incorporated into cover letters and email introductions. Consider adding an anecdote from your experience at a professional event or from a project that helps explain why you were inspired to apply to the opportunity or why you are aligned with the organization's goals and mission.

Example: Incorporating a Memorable Anecdote in a Cover Letter In a *Harvard Business Review* (HBR) article (2022), Elainy Mata interviews HBR editor Amy Gallo for her tips on how to write a job cover letter that gets noticed. During the interview, they work on improving a generic cover letter draft together. After discussing the first half of Elainy's cover letter for a role in video production, which includes an introduction, a brief overview of her relevant skills, and how she would like to contribute to the company's mission, Elainy improved the cover letter by adding a personal anecdote that would be highly relevant to the receiver.

In a middle paragraph of the cover letter, she wrote:

I recently had a chance to try out your Patient Zero product at my current organization. The simulation is both challenging and engaging. I was impressed by your ability to apply different storytelling methods to an online training course (which, let's admit, can often be a little dry). Your work exemplifies exactly what I believe: There's an opportunity to tell a compelling story in everything—all you have to do is deliver it right.

In the interview, Gallo agreed that this was a great approach because it added authenticity, specificity, and personality to what was initially a bland and forgettable cover letter.

Elainy's personal anecdote also passes the five factors of positive memorability. It uses detail, mentioning the receiver's product and simulation; has underlying meaning that the person is familiar with the company's product; is primarily about Elainy; is positive; and is novel. It's unlikely any competitor will share this exact same story.

Start Practicing

Your savviness at becoming memorable comes with practice. If you are introverted, challenge yourself to attend in-person events with a friend and practice introducing yourself to selectors with questions you have prepared in advance. With practice, you'll find that initiating conversations becomes easier and less intimidating. Remind yourself that the selectors who attend events want to meet you!

When developing written cover letters, personal statements, and proposals, try to incorporate relevant memories from your lived experience and go the extra mile to develop and propose novel ideas that draw on your unique knowledge and experiences. Like networking, your writing and idea development skills get better with practice.

Key Takeaways

- Making a positive, memorable impression before or during the application process can help you stand out and make it to the next stage of consideration.
- Anytime you apply to a selective opportunity, find places to create "stickiness" in your written, verbal, or visual outreach that help your name and story last in the mind of the selectors long after they have been introduced to you in person or in writing.
- You can become more memorable to selectors through mutual introductions and self-introductions using "double whammy" questions.
- You can incorporate memorable anecdotes and ideas in your application that incorporate the five factors of positive memorability: they use detail, are novel, have underlying meaning, are primarily about you, and are positive.
- Making a good impression through a memorable approach helps you build your network and reputation over time, leading to word-of-mouth opportunities that come through your network.

Your Turn

Using the selective opportunity you are targeting, identify opportunities to meet your selectors at upcoming events or get an introduction through a mutual contact. To prepare for your introduction and conversation, create in advance a list of "double whammy" questions you can ask that (1) allow you to gather important information about the opportunity that you might not be able to find online and (2) help demonstrate that you are thinking strategically about how you would excel in the opportunity and contribute to the organization's mission.

3

Align Your Mission with Theirs

Win Trust by Championing Their Cause

When I was a senior in college and looking for job opportunities after graduation, I visited the university career office to look for new job postings. This is where I first discovered the world of professional fellowships, when I found a glossy, folded brochure for the New York City Urban Fellows Program. Founded in 1969, NYC Urban Fellows is a prestigious professional fellowship program in New York City government that competitively selects 25 recent graduates from universities across the United States for a nine-month, full-time work placement in a city agency and participation in a series of leadership development seminars.

I didn't know anything like this existed: a high-level apprenticeship for college students like me who were interested in entering a government career track. The stipend was low, but I didn't care. Not only would it place me in New York City, where many of my friends were headed for jobs in finance and consulting, but it would also introduce me to leaders in government and give me a foot in the door for a government job. I immediately imagined myself heading to the Big Apple.

My challenge was that the Urban Fellows program is extremely competitive. A career office staff member told me they get more than 500 applications each year. This got my heart thumping with both excitement and anxiety. I wanted this opportunity badly, and I had only a month to put an application together, including a résumé, personal statement, and three recommendation letters.

I took the brochure with my résumé to my senior advisor at Cornell for advice on how to stand out. The meeting wasn't as optimistic as I had hoped it would be. The professor was happy to write me a recommendation letter but also told me not to get my hopes up because I had only a 3.2 GPA and no internships. He quietly pointed out the competition I faced: I would not only be up against honors students with government internship experience from Cornell, but also top students from all over the country.

Yet again, the message was loud and clear: *you don't stack up to the competition.*

But since I got into Cornell against the odds, I thought I could win my spot in the Urban Fellows program by applying some of the same tactics I used before. I resolved to apply despite the discouragement and be the most prepared applicant in the competition.

A key strategy I used in my Urban Fellows application was *alignment*. To help me stand out as a strong fit, I aimed to show the selectors how my personal mission and goals aligned with their organizational mission.

To do this, I researched what the Urban Fellows' organizational mission and goals were. I was careful not to make any assumptions. My research question was: *why did New York City make an annual investment in recruiting 25 recent graduates from all over the country for a nine-month work placement?*

It wasn't easy to find this information. The NYC Urban Fellows program had a single, outdated webpage of less than 500 words that primarily provided information about the format of the program, eligibility, and the application process. I also had the brochure about the program, but this was equally unhelpful. I didn't have any connections to people who staff the program or people who had won the fellowship that I could talk to. So I primarily used online searches to look for any information I could find about the program, how it works, what impact it makes, and who they select.

Through this research, I came across a press release announcing the most recent class of Fellows, which gave me the answer. In an article, the current program director was quoted talking about the high number of Urban Fellows who go on to become leaders in New York City government years after their fellowship. The article went on to celebrate why the Urban Fellows program was such a great investment for the city.

With this press release, I hit gold. I discovered: *the mission of this program is to create a pipeline of young, talented college graduates who would pursue long-term careers in NYC government.*

This mission meant a number of things for how I would craft my application story.

First, it meant that I should express my strong alignment with the program's goals: a desire to establish a long-term career in NYC government. Second, the career goal stated in my application should not be something out of alignment, like a desire to use the program as a gap year before graduate school or a goal to work at the federal level in Washington, DC.

Finally, the program's mission signaled to me that they would probably select some candidates who had a personal connection to New York City—something I didn't have. They might also be looking for candidates with some experience working in government through summer internships—another thing I did not have.

However, I hoped that more important than NYC connections or internship experience would be a sincere commitment to pursuing a career in public service—something I *did* have. I majored in government in college, I had an authentic desire to work in New York City government, and I had an interest in applying my talents to urban challenges in education based on my personal experience attending an under-resourced public high school. I also had four years of significant volunteer and work-study experience through the student-led organization On-Site Volunteer Services in Ithaca that demonstrated my commitment to public service.

So that's exactly what I told them in my Urban Fellows application. And it worked. The strength of my career goal alignment got me a finalist interview—but I was still a big step away from selection.

Thinking back to the possibility that they might preference candidates with knowledge of New York City, I read the *New York Times* every day leading up to the full-day interview. Consequently, I was highly prepared to showcase my critical thinking skills and knowledge of New York City government. When put on the spot in an awkward group interview where they asked all the finalists to discuss solutions to a city policy challenge while the selectors observed, I was able to readily speak to current New York City policy initiatives, partners, and resources at a level of detail none of the other candidates displayed. I'm certain this extra preparation for the interview cinched my selection for the 2001–2002 cohort of New York City Urban Fellows.

The mission of the NYC Urban Fellows program may have changed since 2000, but even today, the website does not have a clear mission statement. It does say, "Urban Fellows are placed at an array of agencies across the City where they learn about public policy and work closely with leaders engaged in policy and operational work" (nyc.gov 2025). This statement might lead you to believe the program exists to help you achieve your personal ambition of receiving professional and leadership development. Don't be fooled by this vague statement! The NYC Urban Fellows remains an important tool for

NYC to attract and retain the nation's top college graduates for long-term careers in city government service.

As I applied to competitive programs and awards throughout my career, I made an effort to research the program's mission and goals to show how my personal mission aligns with their organizational mission. This approach contributed greatly to my success throughout my career as I edged out candidates who had higher GPAs, more work experience, higher job titles, and more accolades.

My approach exemplifies the letter *A* in the MATCH ME Formula®, which stands for *Aligns with the organization's mission*. **The purpose of demonstrating alignment in your pitch is to show that you understand the organization's mission and care about helping them advance their mission.**

In this chapter, you will learn:

- Why mission alignment matters
- What an organization's mission is (and is not)
- Ways to identify an organization's mission and current goals
- How to refine your personal mission
- How to show mission alignment in your job, graduate school, investment, or award application to help you stand out

Why Mission Alignment Matters

Every single organization on the planet wants to choose people who are not just smart and ambitious but who also understand and are enthusiastic about helping them achieve their mission and goals. An organization would never knowingly select a candidate who does not care about their mission.

Your degree of care about an organization's mission is reflected in the alignment with your personal mission to make a social impact. Your personal mission alignment is the one thing that will indicate whether you will be a trusted, satisfied, and productive member of the team in the future, including when the organization faces challenges, because you are intrinsically motivated to help them achieve their mission. For this reason, the alignment of your personal mission with the organization's mission is more important to selectors than your skills, work experience, GPA, or previous accolades.

Mission alignment is especially important when you have very little experience in the field of the opportunity, worry that you may be considered underqualified or overqualified, or have a professional or academic background that is varied and difficult to summarize.

I learned about the power of mission alignment through my experience successfully applying to opportunities where I edged out candidates with more experience and credentials and, later, my experience of assessing and hiring candidates for roles in my own organization. Here are two examples that demonstrate the importance of alignment over other attributes:

- **When mission alignment is more important than skills:** Let's say you are a computer engineer and also an environmental activist who publishes articles on the negative consequences of pollution from fossil fuels in your free time. It's unlikely you would be hired by a large oil company for a role on their engineering team even if you are the very best engineer on the market. Based on your personal activities, they would doubt you have a sincere interest in helping them achieve their corporate goals and might assume you could work against them while publishing articles on pollution.
- **When mission alignment is more important than years of work experience and accolades:** Let's say you have spent your entire career in academia as a professor and have published several award-winning textbooks on American history. After a career break to raise children, you decide to change careers and apply to a mid-level journalism position at a local news outlet. You assume you will be a top candidate because you have more

than 15 years of experience in writing, research, and publication, as well as awards. Yet, if you don't explain how you align with the mission and goals of the local news outlet, it's unlikely you'll be considered. They will assume this is a temporary plan and that you'll leave once you find a more aligned opportunity in academia where your experience is based.

To be successful, it's not enough to believe you are aligned and a great fit for the opportunity; you must state the alignment explicitly in your pitch to give selectors the information they need to choose you. This means you must deeply understand what their mission and goals are, have a clear definition of your personal mission, and effectively express how these missions are mutually reinforcing.

What the Organization's Mission Is

An organization's mission is its approach to solving problems, with supporting goals that define the scope of its impact. Every type of organization has a primary mission and several goals that support that mission:

- **Companies** create and sell products and services that solve problems for their customers and have a goal to generate revenue and make a profit while doing so.
- **Nonprofit and government organizations** have both a mission and a responsibility to solve problems through the services they provide. They also have a goal to achieve enough funding to sustain their work.
- **Universities** offer degrees, which I liken to training; their mission is to train people for specific career tracks by providing higher education. Universities also have a goal to be recognized for research output and high-quality teaching in order to attract research funding and top talent.
- **Fellowship organizations** aim to solve social problems by investing in the career advancement of emerging and

established leaders and scholars. Depending on the organization, some also have a mission to create greater gender or racial diversity in an industry, build communities of practice, bring attention to certain issues, or fill research gaps, among others.
- **Business accelerators and investors** aim to support a thriving entrepreneurial ecosystem that helps start-ups get off the ground. They also help capitalists identify companies poised to be profitable so that they can make a high return on their investment.

While each organization has a social mission and approach that is unique to them, generally, their mission will fall within these broad definitions.

What the Organization's Mission Is Not

When you start to research organizations, you'll notice that an organization's mission has nothing to do with helping you achieve needs and desires that serve only you. While these may be an outcome of an opportunity they offer and even used as a marketing tool for recruiting talent, there is always a broader social mission unrelated to your personal ambition to be paid, fulfilled, titled, or recognized.

To be clear:

- Jobs do not exist to give people a paycheck because people have bills to pay; they exist to execute the organization's solution to a problem that serves others.
- University degree programs do not exist to satiate people who love to learn; they exist to prepare and credential people for specific careers and outcomes.
- Awards do not exist to help someone look prestigious and receive media attention; they exist to spotlight efforts and accomplishments that serve the broader industry.
- Capitalists do not invest in start-ups to help entrepreneurs achieve their dream of starting a business; they invest to generate a financial return on their investment.

Yet, time and time again, I have seen candidates answer the question "Why you?" with the achievement of a self-centric need or desire as the primary reason why they are applying and why they should be selected. I see job candidates tell hiring managers that they are applying to a leadership position because they are seeking a higher title and pay, and university applicants say they should be selected because it would be an honor to be the first in their family to attend college. Although these common responses are believed to sound compelling, they fail to address the organization's mission and how you will help them achieve their goals.

Within Western societies, ambition and financial success are highly valued, and so we have been coached from childhood to express our personal ambitions when applying to competitive opportunities. Yet, when you use your self-centric goal as your primary reason for pursuing an opportunity, it falls flat because it lacks consideration for the needs of the giver. It implies that you did not make an effort to understand what the organization is trying to achieve now and in the future and, perhaps, don't care. That impression is a recipe for rejection.

So keep that in mind as you aim to show alignment in your application. The organizations that offer selective jobs, university spots, and awards are in the power position and should be the "hero" in your application. They have options, and in almost all cases, you need them more than they need you.

What they care about most is achieving their organizational goals in the most effective way possible, and they will pick and invest in people whom they feel are the most likely to help them do that. The more candidates they have to choose from, the more critical it is that you are highly aligned with their organizational goals, bolstered with evidence from your background that you'll be committed and successful if you are selected.

How to Demonstrate Mission Alignment

If you know the mission and goals of the organization offering the job, degree, award, or opportunity of interest, you can ensure you are spending time applying to the right opportunities for you and create the strongest possible pitch. I recommend you apply only to opportunities that have a mission that you are fully aligned with and that you authentically desire.

Before a personal statement or a cover letter is written or an introduction is made, you've got to do your research on the organization's mission and goals. This may take a few hours to a few weeks (and your time may be limited if you have only a brief window of time to apply). In any case, the more time you have for this research, the better!

Once you have done enough research on the organization's mission to confirm the opportunity is right for you, you can prepare an application that shows the selectors that you understand their most aspirational goals and would be committed and instrumental in helping them advance their mission.

Interestingly, it can sometimes be challenging to identify an organization's mission and goals by looking at its website. This is where mission research comes into play. It's an approach that can help you get inside the mind of the selection committee to identify what they are really looking for in candidates.

Research the Organization's Mission

When you set out to identify the mission and goals of an organization, your guiding questions should be:

- What problems do they solve?
- What approaches, products, and solutions do they sell or offer?
- How do they generate revenue or outside funding to do their work?
- What networks and areas of influence do they create?
- What new goals are they addressing in the next 12 months?
- What are the impact aspirations of the individuals on the leadership team?

The following are a few places where you can start gathering this research online.

Mission Statements and Goals To begin, seek language on the organization's website about its mission and goals. Some organizations have this information front and center in a "mission statement." A mission statement might be in the website menu bar, but it also might be located on the home page, on an "About" page, or on a page labeled "What We Do" or "Who We Are."

A few examples:

- Forbes' mission statement, placed on a page titled "Who We Are" (Forbes 2025), states, "Forbes gives people the knowledge, resources, inspiration, and connections they need to achieve success."
- On the U.S. Department of Education's website (2025), their mission statement is "To promote student achievement and preparation for global competitiveness by fostering educational excellence and ensuring equal access."
- The Gates Foundation website (2025) says, "Our mission is to create a world where every person has the opportunity to live a healthy, productive life."
- Tesla's website (2025) states it has "one mission," which is "We're building a world powered by solar energy, running on batteries and transported by electric vehicles."

When you look at mission statements like these from organizations offering opportunities, ask yourself: *do I care about these goals and approaches?*

If yes, you are seeking opportunities in the right place.

As you can see, mission statements are often broad and vague, and some organizations don't have a published mission statement at all, so don't stop there with your research.

Values Statements   Look for website language that expresses what the organization aims to achieve and the values that support those goals. ProFellow® has a clear values statement for the primary problem it aims to solve: making elite educational and leadership opportunities more accessible and transparent. On a page entitled "About ProFellow" (ProFellow 2025), the company defines its values as follows:

> *Our Values:*
>
> - We believe in knowledge sharing.
> - We believe in the power of positive support.
> - We believe in leveling the playing field.
> - We believe in paying it forward.

When you find an organization's values statement, ask yourself: *do I care about these values?*

If they align with your personal values, you are on the right track.

Competitor Differentiators   Another way to identify an organization's mission and goals is to find language that explains how the organization is different from its competitors. If you can understand how they approach and solve problems differently, you can find unique alignment, especially if those differences excite you.

Jim Burke Ford, a Ford Motor Company reseller based in Bakersfield, California, made it clear on its website (Jim Burke Ford 2025) why Ford cars are better than the competition. In a page giving an overview of "Ford vs. GMC," the company states:

> *One benefit Ford has over GMC is that the company offers more options, giving Bakersfield consumers a wider variety of trucks and SUVs to choose from. With Ford, drivers can find multiple gas and hybrid options, but GMC doesn't offer hybrid vehicles, and the company has fewer gas-powered models in its lineup.*

If you were seeking a role at Ford Motor Company, you would ask yourself: *Do these differentiators matter to me, and do they align with my values? Could I see myself promoting these differentiators on behalf of the organization?*

Another example from the higher education industry is how graduate schools and degree programs differentiate themselves, particularly in their marketing materials. William & Mary offers undergraduate and master's degrees in history. In a web page with the subheading "What Makes Us Different" (William & Mary 2025), William & Mary defines its differentiators clearly, including:

- *Award-Winning Faculty:* Many W&M faculty members have won some of the most prestigious awards for teaching, scholarship and general excellence.
- *Proximity to the "Historic Triangle":* Study resources from American history in the places they were found.
- *The Clem History Writing Center:* Consult with advanced Ph.D. candidates on research and writing assignments. Explore the handouts filled with tips and tricks for strong writing.
- *Pipeline to Higher Learning:* W&M's most successful undergraduates have recently been admitted to highly selective doctoral and professional programs.

If you are researching degree programs and looking at their differentiators, ask yourself: *Are these differentiators important to me? Do these differentiators matter to me more than other types of program features, and why?*

Press Releases and News Features Press releases and news features are excellent places to find out what organizations are trying to achieve in the near future. Current news pieces can share both the organization's well-known mission and goals, as well as announcements about their lesser-known, cutting-edge initiatives that will be supported through new funding, innovations, or partnerships. Company news articles might contain useful information about the direction the company is moving in, which an applicant can use to show mission alignment.

For example, AI is on everyone's lips at the moment. AI technology is advancing so quickly that every company is in a race to figure out how to use AI to give them a competitive advantage and not lose their market share. If you are applying for positions at tech companies, look closely at recent press releases to understand how they are incorporating new technologies and generate ideas for how you would want to support their future approach. Information about new investments, pilot projects, and initiatives may not be on their primary website yet, so many of your competitors will miss these rapidly changing company insights. Your mention of the company's most recent goals and initiatives can make you stand out, demonstrating you're a serious applicant who's done your research.

I encourage graduate school applicants to read the school's recent press releases in the "News" section of the website, which might be the only place where an applicant can find announcements about recent grant awards faculty have received or new projects or curricula the school is launching. With this information, you can express research and study interests in your application that are in alignment with the school's future research and teaching initiatives, helping you to stand out among candidates who did not look at these upcoming projects.

Who They Selected in the Past When applying to competitive cohort-based programs like graduate schools, fellowships, and business accelerators, you can also identify the program's mission by identifying themes in the backgrounds and projects of the cohorts of people they selected in the recent past. The demographics of those they selected in the past signal the types of people they will likely select in the future, which is helpful to know when the program's eligibility guidelines are broad or vague. This research will help you identify if you are the right fit because the program is designed to meet your needs, as well as avoid opportunities that are a poor fit because they choose people who are very different from you.

For example, imagine you are 28 years old and interested in a "midcareer" leadership program. Through research of past cohorts, you see that the organization typically picks C-suite executives in their 40s. To get picked, you'll need to effectively explain why the program is the right step for someone of your age and experience level. If you're an extraordinary person who has made it to the C-suite at age 28, you can make a strong case! On the other hand, if you have progressive experience but are not yet C-suite, it's going to be hard to show why you are a good fit. Bookmark the program for a later application.

Likewise, imagine you are a midcareer professional in your 40s aiming to make a career change to work in public service, and you are excited to find a professional fellowship in local government that doesn't have an explicit age limit. But in looking at the previous fellowship cohorts, you find they exclusively select recent college graduates in their 20s. Why do they select only recent graduates and not people of a variety of ages? The answer lies in the program's mission to support recent graduates in launching their careers. This mission may not be stated on their website, but it is implicit in who they select.

Additional Sources Beyond the organization's website and articles, you can find even deeper information about their primary and supplementary goals from white papers, annual reports, presentations they give, conferences they attend, company and leadership newsletters, and corporate and philanthropic sponsorships.

Supplementary goals are things like creating an inclusive workplace culture or working with local partners to contribute to the region's economic vitality. Take note of these supplementary goals and objectives because they offer additional opportunities to show alignment.

Some questions you should explore include:

- **Stakeholder engagement:** How is the organization engaging with its stakeholders, including customers, partners, and policymakers? Do they have a strong focus on customer service or advancing social priorities?
- **Reputation building:** How is the organization advancing its reputation for quality services and products? What conferences do they sponsor or attend?
- **Philanthropy:** What causes does the organization support or donate to?
- **Goals of the leadership team:** What is the background of the organization's individual leadership, and what issues do they care about? Do they publish thought leadership content related or unrelated to the organization's mission?

In doing this deeper research, you might find a lesser-known organizational goal that you find incredibly important and exciting. The goals you find most aligned with your interests are those you can emphasize in the statement of your mission alignment.

Use mission research to help you narrow down opportunities to ones where you can explain from the perspective of the selection committee why you would be selected because of your alignment. Being eligible to apply for an opportunity is not the same as being a good fit. You can be the youngest or the oldest person they have ever selected, or the most unique or interdisciplinary, but in all cases, your selection must align with the organization's mission and the outcomes they want to achieve.

With all of this gathered information, you should have a crystallized understanding of what they do, who they select, and why. This information will help you decide if the opportunity is fully aligned with your background and goals. If it is, you now have the ingredients to begin building a detailed and compelling answer to the question "Why you?"

After completing your mission research, the next step is to define your personal mission so that you can draw parallels between your mission and theirs.

Define Your Personal Mission

What is your personal mission? This question is important to answer because alignment happens when your personal mission aligns with the organization's mission.

A personal mission is your pursuit of a goal that helps solve a problem experienced by others. Your personal mission might be to advance scientific research, build products that people love, advocate for justice, improve local economies, teach and mentor, defend your country, treat illness, create art, inspire others to succeed, and so much more.

In defining your personal mission, ask yourself:

- Who do you want to help?
- What problems do you want to help solve?
- What initiatives do you want to contribute to?
- What kind of legacy do you want to leave for the next generation?

Think *we*, not *me*.

In reality, your personal mission is unlikely to be a single, permanent goal. Over the course of your career, your personal mission can change as you undertake different professional and academic roles and volunteer your time for causes you care about. Sometimes, you might have multiple personal missions because you have lots of interests and are involved in a wide variety of professional, academic, and personal activities.

To be selected for a competitive opportunity, however, you must express in your application or pitch a singular personal mission that aligns with the organization's mission. Being vague about your personal mission or expressing lots of different interests and personal goals at once is confusing and will put you at a disadvantage. It makes it hard for the selectors to visualize the future you and how you will operate if you are selected. A selector might conclude you lack focus and are noncommittal.

For example, when I was in college as a government major, I did not have a specific personal mission or career goal. Broadly, I had a desire to work in public service and apply my talents and skills to whatever problems needed me. From taking a wide range of liberal arts classes and studying abroad, I had interests all over the map that prompted me to apply to many different entry-level jobs and fellowships, including positions in education policy, public health, international affairs, K-12 teaching, and social work. To be honest, I was a little lost about what path to pursue; I just knew I wanted to do work that was socially impactful and interesting.

But I knew I shouldn't let this uncertainty about my career path seep into my applications because it would confuse my application story and hurt my ability to stand out among other contenders who were confidently expressing a very specific and aligned goal. So each time I applied for an opportunity, I narrowed my personal mission and career goal to something highly specific in order to show my alignment with the organization's mission.

When I applied to the NYC Urban Fellows program, there were a hundred possible career paths I could have taken after graduation; working in NYC government was just one possible path. But the Urban Fellows application was not a place to muse about all the possible paths I was open to. If I sounded noncommittal about working in NYC government long term, I would have appeared misaligned with the organization's mission. To sound focused, I made it *the* path for the purpose of my application.

I got into the Urban Fellows program using an aligned career goal, but ultimately, I stayed in NYC government for only two years before undertaking a fellowship in Germany and making my way to policy work at the federal level in Washington, DC. As my career unfolded, it took me in a different direction as new interests and opportunities arose.

I was pleasantly surprised to find there was no negative consequence to changing my career direction after my fellowship. Today, I am engaged as an alumna of the NYC Urban Fellows program and continue to work in public service. The Urban Fellows staff remained great colleagues who supported the shifts I made as I changed careers because they care about people above all else. You'll experience this support yourself when you work for companies, organizations, and universities that have compassionate leaders.

So don't be afraid to refine your personal mission to one specific goal and area of impact for the purpose of creating a clear and compelling application story for a selective opportunity. You can have many other interests and possible paths; most applicants do. Just choose one personal mission that is aligned and authentic, and work to make your personal mission as clear and specific as possible in your application.

If you are still unsure how to define your personal mission for an opportunity you are interested in, look at the organization's mission and begin to jot out a refined personal mission statement that is aligned using their own language. Consider the following:

- Why you care about the organization's mission and the problems they aim to solve
- The evidence that demonstrates you care about the problems they aim to solve, such as your choice of academic studies, choice of jobs, volunteer roles you've undertaken, expertise you have developed, and more
- How you would uniquely contribute to their mission and their approach by applying your specific skills, perspectives, and talents
- How the opportunity will help you achieve your personal mission for social impact on others in the future and if the opportunity allows you to make an impact at a greater scale than you are making now

> **Tip: A career or academic goal that is me-centric is not a personal mission.**
>
> This **is not** a personal mission (*me-centric*): *I want to achieve a graduate degree at your university because your institution's prestigious reputation will help me land a well-paid position at a top pharmaceutical company.*
>
> This **is** a personal mission (*we-centric*): *I want to achieve a graduate degree at your university because it will provide the curriculum and skills development I need to develop innovative research on cancer therapies in my future role as a research director.*
>
> © Pitch Your Potential / Vicki Johnson, Ph.D.

Show Mission Alignment

You have now identified the organization's mission through investigative research, and you find it aligns closely with your personal mission. This is where the magic comes in.

When you are highly aligned with an opportunity, you will be able to express that you understand the problems the organization is trying to solve and why you support their unique approach. You can demonstrate your mission alignment by explaining in detail how you can contribute to their mission and how these actions will help you achieve your personal mission, often expressed as a career goal. In written applications and in interviews, it's important to be highly specific, a strategy I will discuss in more detail in Chapter 6.

The best place to show your alignment is through the expression of your aligned career goal and the social impact you want to make in the future. Through a highly specific career goal tailored to the opportunity, you can explicitly show how your goals and ideas would help produce the desired outcome of the organization's mission.

Case Study: Creating Mission Alignment Expertly Someone who became an expert at creating mission alignment in her competitive applications is Rachel Santarsiero, a long-time member of the ProFellow community who became a ProFellow coach after winning multiple fellowships and graduate school acceptances. When I first met Rachel, she had just graduated from college with a degree in civil engineering and was working at a civil engineering firm. But Rachel's real passion was in international affairs and the Arabic language. She discovered the world of international fellowships in college and applied to many exciting opportunities, including a Fulbright award to Morocco. However, she faced rejections at first and assumed it was because she majored in engineering and was a weak candidate for international awards. In working together, she learned that her unique background in engineering was an asset, not a disadvantage; she just needed to better align her personal mission for social impact in international affairs with the funding body's mission.

While in graduate school, Rachel expressed mission alignment expertly in her application for funding from the National Churchill Library Center (NCLC) to conduct her thesis fieldwork in Morocco. It was a bit of a long shot because the NCLC grant was not specific to funding research work in the Middle East, but Rachel found a compelling connection between her personal mission and goals and the organization's current goals to elevate women's studies. In her statement of interest, she wrote:

> *My current research focuses on indigenous women in Imider, Morocco, to understand their role in advocating for water rights and show how nonnormative, gendered forms of protest can combat environmental degradation. Through conversations with Program Director Justin Reash, I understand that NCLC is committed to elevating disciplines like women's studies; my research presents an exciting opportunity to expand this scholarship.*

Just as I aim to elevate the voices of indigenous women, Winston Churchill, too, understood the importance of surrounding himself with women's voices. During the 1945 Yalta Conference, Churchill attended the pivotal event accompanied by his daughter, Sarah Churchill. Sarah was devoted to her father, and Churchill depended on Sarah's astute and political mind. Catherine Grace Katz writes about this in "The Daughters of Yalta" and, through archival research, tells the little-known story of the sentimentality and loyalty shown by Sarah, Anna Roosevelt, and Kathleen Harriman during the conference—and their role in defining the post-war world alongside their fathers. Like Katz, my research highlights Churchill's example by elevating the unique role that women play alongside men in solving global problems.

You can see how Rachel compared the personal mission of Winston Churchill and the organizational mission of the NCLC with her personal mission to advance women's empowerment through research. This created a unique and memorable expression of mission alignment that landed her the award.

Rachel also expertly used mission alignment in her successful applications to Ph.D. and master's programs. In the case of graduate school, mission alignment is the alignment of your academic and career goals with the graduate program's training mission.

In her personal statement to a master's program at Worcester Polytechnic Institute, where she was not only accepted but also achieved a full funding award, she expressed alignment with the program's mission to train students for careers in global development and international security. In this excerpt, Rachel explains in high detail the unique benefits of the graduate program and how she would capitalize on them, and she ends the paragraph with her career goal. She wrote:

My diverse interests, user-centered design philosophy, and love of Arabic culture have all led me to pursue a Master in Science and Technology for

Innovation and Global Development at WPI. I plan to take classes within the Society, Technology, and Policy Program (STP) at WPI, and the International Development, Community, and Environment Program (IDCE) at Clark to design a curriculum that focuses on forced migration due to climate change within the Middle East and North Africa (MENA) region. Not only will the coursework prepare me for this, but the WPI Development Design Lab will be a key resource in enacting social change and supportive policy development. . . . After my time at WPI, I plan to continue my research in climate migration by working with an NGO that integrates climate change measures into policies, strategies, and planning.

As you write your application text to describe your mission alignment, follow Rachel's example in the case study provided by emphasizing your personal mission for positive impact on others, not just your personal ambitions to achieve a higher job title, pay, or prestige. Your personal ambitions are important because the strength of your personal ambitions can reflect the strength of your work ethic, self-confidence, and commitment to achieving success, but ultimately, the organization will choose the person who is most aligned with their goals.

Your Personal Mission Is a Journey, Not a Destination

Researching the organization's mission is a tactic to help you identify great opportunities for you and create an exceptional application by incorporating mission alignment. It should also help you avoid pursuing opportunities that are a poor fit. Be honest with yourself through the process of mission research. There are many exciting jobs, fellowships, awards, and graduate school opportunities, but don't become a victim of shiny object syndrome. You can waste a lot of time and effort forcing a square peg (you) into a round hole (them). Don't apply to opportunities that are misaligned with your background and personal mission just to look successful to others or to fill a superficial need while knowing you won't enjoy the work. If you do, you may get accepted, but it's unlikely you'll feel purpose in your day-to-day activities.

If you are still feeling lost and lacking a personal mission, use mission research of jobs, fellowships, and other opportunities that spark your interest to identify the groups that are seeking the skills and talent that you have. Focus on the problems that those organizations are solving and define an authentic personal mission around the problems that excite you most. Mission research on competitive opportunities can help you identify problems that are priorities for others, which is a great place to start.

If you find an aligned opportunity but are concerned that you won't be competitive because you are less experienced or credentialed than those the organization typically picks, be careful not to discount your competitiveness. Mission alignment matters more than years of work experience and credentials. If you have big ideas and know that you can make a contribution, ignore the naysayers externally and in your mind, as I did. If you have a strong mission alignment and know that you can contribute a high degree of skill, creativity, and expertise, challenge yourself and apply! Even if you face rejection, each aspirational opportunity you apply to is a chance to practice your persuasive writing and interview skills and further define your story and personal mission. The process also allows you to get your name and face in front of influential people and build your network. This practice of applying to highly aligned opportunities will invariably bring you closer to the right opportunities and greater success in the future.

Key Takeaways

- The organization's mission is their approach to addressing the problems they want to solve. Your personal mission is your pursuit of a goal that helps solve a problem experienced by

others. A key strategy for success is to align your personal mission with the organization's mission.
- Your personal mission alignment is more important to selectors than your skills, work experience, GPA, and previous accolades. If you are highly aligned with the organization's mission, the more likely it is that you will be successful in the role; if your alignment is weak or unclear, selectors will assume you are less likely to thrive.
- Before beginning an application, deeply research the organization's mission and goals on their website by looking for a stated mission statement, values statements, and competitor differentiators.
- To identify the organization's immediate goals and challenges and new initiatives that are not yet on their website, look for this information in press releases, media, conference presentations, and newsletters.
- For cohort-based opportunities, look for themes in who they have selected in the past to find a mission that is implicit in who they choose to invest in.
- Narrow your personal mission to something that is specific and aligned with the organization's mission. You can show mission alignment in the expression of your highly specific career goal or with the inclusion of an innovative idea.
- You'll have the most success applying to opportunities where you have strong mission alignment. Bypass opportunities where you don't.

Your Turn

Using the selective opportunity you are targeting, do your research on the organization's mission and goals. Search online for mission and values statements, competitor differentiators, news features, and reports. For cohort-based programs, look for themes among those they selected in the past. Create a document with answers to these questions:

- What is their mission statement?
- What problems do they solve?
- What approaches, products, and solutions do they execute or sell?
- How do they generate revenue or donor funding to do their work?
- What networks and areas of influence do they have now and do they aim to build?
- What new goals are they addressing in the next 12 months?
- What are the aspirations of the individuals on the leadership team?

Once you have found their mission and goals and have a good sense of what they are trying to achieve now and in the near future, draft a few sentences that explain why your personal mission is aligned with the organization's mission. Start with these guiding questions:

- Why do you care about their mission and goals?
- What problems related to their mission and goals do you want to help solve in the future?
- What would the future look like if you were able to help them achieve their mission and goals and make a positive impact on others?
- What would be the scope of your impact on their mission if you are selected?
- How could helping them advance their mission also advance your skills, expertise and experiences, and career trajectory?

4 | Make Your Goals **Timely**

Prove Your Impact Can't Wait

When I was a young professional working at a public health professional association in Washington, DC, I unexpectedly had the chance to be a "fly on the wall" when a group of managers was reviewing and discussing the applications they received for a competitive summer internship at the organization. The internship was an opportunity for a graduate student to work at the association over the summer and access some of our center's resources and datasets for research toward their dissertation. The intern would also contribute to association activities just like a member of the staff and would attend association events.

While sitting at my desk, I opened an email blast sent two hours before, inviting all the staff to come by and eat the leftover food from a meeting in our main conference room. Hoping to grab some cookies and coffee, I came down the hall and knocked quietly on the open door.

Three program managers, one of whom was my boss, were having a small meeting at the other end of the room. They smiled and nodded for me to come in and help myself.

As I was loading up my paper plate with my back to them, they started to discuss something that caught my attention.

"June is excellent. I'm certain she'll be successful. Her reference letters are strong. But I don't know how we distinguish her from Carmen, who is equally excellent. This is a hard decision!" said my boss, laughing.

"Yeah," said another selector. "But let's consider this. Carmen mentioned in her application that she would like to attend the regional conference with us this July so she can meet people for professional networking. That's a very good opportunity for her. She is in the final year of her Ph.D. and will be on the job market soon."

"Yes, good point," my boss responded. "But maybe June has more to learn and gain from the internship because she's only in the third year of her Ph.D. program?"

"I'm also leaning toward Carmen for another reason," said the third selector. "The research that she is working on is very timely, looking at social determinants of health inequalities. That is the theme of this year's conference. Professionally, she would be missing out on this opportunity if she didn't have another way to attend."

My boss chimed in. "You know ... we could encourage June to apply again next year; she has two more shots while in grad school." The conversation paused. I think heads were nodding.

They discussed June versus Carmen for a bit longer. I tried to appear busy pouring coffee so I could continue eavesdropping. Long story short, it was decided: Carmen was selected for the internship.

Listening to this conversation unfold was fascinating to me because it validated something that I had a hunch about for many years: timeliness can give you just the edge you need to be chosen over other finalists.

With selective opportunities, there are always more qualified candidates than spots available, so it's advantageous to find every opportunity to give yourself an edge (or several). I learned through experimentation in my applications that one way to stand out is to express why your selection is timely and urgent by explaining why you need the organization's resources for achieving your personal mission right now.

A pitch that is timely includes ideas for outcomes that are important and relevant to people and problems now, not those in the past or far future. Timeliness includes urgency, a strong reason why you need this opportunity now and might relinquish a time-limited benefit if you are not selected.

The story of June and Carmen exemplifies the letter *T* in the MATCH ME Formula®, which stands for *Timely*. **Making a pitch that is timely, expressing reasons why your selection should not be delayed, helps make the selectors the "hero" in your application story.** An application story that is timely can give you an edge when all other candidate factors are equal.

In this chapter, you will learn:

- Why timeliness matters
- How to demonstrate timeliness by incorporating current events in your pitch
- How to demonstrate timeliness through urgency

Why Timeliness Matters

Every organization has a variety of problems they are addressing, but they will have a short list of priority problems that need a solution now, not later. The timeliness of the ideas for impact that you include in your application can be a powerful tool to show why you are the best pick.

For cohort-based opportunities like fellowships, graduate programs, and business accelerators, timeliness is also an important factor because they will assess if your proposed project, research, or business idea could gain media and industry attention, outside sources of funding, and the buy-in of the organization's key stakeholders.

While you may be up against other contenders who are seemingly more accomplished or qualified than you, they may miss the mark if they pitch ideas that do not address the organization's current priorities. An applicant can also miss the mark by proposing ideas that are too early because the organization does not yet have the resources, team, or influence to execute them in the next 12 months. When candidates rely solely on organizations' static website information to prepare for applications and interviews, they often miss information on the most current events that are impacting the members of the selection committee in their day-to-day jobs.

Your application story is timely when you can answer "Why you?" with an example of how you will advance the organization's current priority goals—not their past goals or goals that are not yet top priorities. After undertaking your mission research, you should have a deep understanding of what the organization is trying to achieve in the next 12 months so you are in a better position to discuss how your selection will address their most pressing and current challenges.

When you do this skillfully, using information found in less obvious places, you can sometimes create a mirage of being "telepathic"— demonstrating your knowledge of the organization's latest happenings that are not yet in mainstream media. This can help differentiate you from other candidates who did not research the organization deeply.

Likewise, when you are applying for funding to support a project, research, or a business idea, the more timely your work, the more successful it will be in obtaining resources. Projects that are timely are more likely to get the attention of stakeholders, investors, and media.

Demonstrate Timeliness by Incorporating Current Events

The organization's most pressing challenges and new goals unfolding now and in the immediate future may be hidden in less obvious places, such as recent company newsletters, news and press releases, interviews with leadership, and conference presentations. When you find and leverage this information, you can pitch your potential in helping the organization address those priority challenges and goals, which is an approach that your competitors may not take.

How to be timely in your application will depend in large part on the type of opportunity involved, as illustrated here:

- **A corporate job opening:** Show the selection committee that you have an area of expertise, a skill set, a network of people, or an innovative idea that will feasibly help the company address its most pressing challenge within the next 12 months.

    Example: Imagine you are a software engineer applying for a role at a top technology company. As part of your mission research and application prep, you watch a webinar from a recent tech conference where a member of the company's sales team discusses how the company is incorporating AI into their product line and plans to release new features in the near future. As an experienced engineer, you know these changes are not easy to make. Citing this presentation, discuss your ideas for leveraging technologies that you have expertise in that will help them iterate faster and retain their market share against new competitors. Even if the idea you pose is not perfect because it is based on limited external information, you will demonstrate that you did your research on the company in less obvious places to understand the market challenges the company is currently facing.

- **A government or nonprofit job opening:** Show the selection committee that you can help address the most current challenges that are impacting their service mission.

    Example: Imagine you are an experienced program manager applying for a program director role at a large nonprofit organization addressing early education initiatives. As part of your mission research and application prep, you read the organization's recent philanthropic newsletter where they quietly share the news that they raised less money at their annual gala than the previous year. In your interview for the role, mention that you read their recent newsletter and share your ideas for doing more with fewer resources. Even if some of your proposed ideas are already being executed or are not feasible, you will have demonstrated that you care enough about the organization to pay close attention to their newsletter and, more importantly, that you are aware of and ready to lead through this recent financial turbulence.

- **Graduate school:** Discuss in your personal statement how graduate school will help you enter a career track that addresses a timely social challenge. You can also propose dissertation research on a subject that addresses a timely challenge or priority research gap identified by external organizations.

    Example: Imagine you are applying to top master's programs in international affairs and your career goal is to become a U.S. Foreign Service Officer (FSO). In your application, you can discuss how some of the program's specific coursework will give you knowledge and skills to become an effective FSO and address the most pressing diplomatic challenges now, such as the Israeli-Palestinian conflict, infectious disease control in developing countries, and refugee crises caused by climate-driven natural disasters.

- **Business investment:** Emphasize to investors and selective business accelerators how your business idea helps solve a current societal challenge and will have increasing demand.

    Example: Imagine you and your health tech company co-founder are applying to Y Combinator, a start-up business accelerator that offers each selected company experienced mentorship and $500,000 in venture capital. In your application, you can discuss how your business idea will capitalize on new trends and interest in precision medicine by utilizing AI. Show how the technology is not only timely, but the business model will prioritize therapies for heart disease, which has been identified as the most costly challenge in healthcare today.

Case Study: Proposing a Timely Project From my own experience, proposing a timely project was the primary factor for my selection for the German Chancellor Fellowship sponsored by the Alexander von Humboldt Foundation. In the early 2000s, this prestigious professional fellowship annually selected 10 Americans and 10 Russians up to age 40 through a competitive application process to spend a year in Germany focused on a professional project of their own design. Because of its association with the German Chancellor and its generous financial and immersion language support, the fellowship was very competitive.

I came across this program in my Internet searches for fellowships after spending a year as a New York City Urban Fellow supporting the NYC Office of Emergency Management during the recovery operation from the 2001 World Trade Center attacks (9/11). I never expected to find a fellowship that would not only allow me to live abroad in Europe for a year and study a new language but also have the autonomy to focus on a project that I designed. It was a unique and exciting opportunity for someone like me who thought that studying abroad was only for students.

Because most of the candidates they selected had 5–15 years of work experience and a graduate degree, I wasn't sure I would be considered a strong candidate having only a bachelor's, no German language experience, and only a year and a half of professional experience in New York City government when I applied. I was 24 years old.

But I reasoned that I had a unique opportunity to propose a project that was timely and attention-grabbing because I was working at the epicenter of the 9/11 response and recovery operation, an event that engaged the globe and continued to impact global security, foreign diplomacy, and emergency preparedness measures. I had just spent one year working for the NYC Office of Emergency Management, and at the time of my application, I had moved to a new position at the NYC Department of Health and Mental Hygiene (DOHMH), where I worked on bioterrorism preparedness efforts. It was a fast-paced agency grappling with new challenges. In 2001, the United States also experienced an unidentified anthrax attack through powdered anthrax sent through the U.S. mail, causing 22 anthrax cases and five deaths. These events fundamentally changed the role of public health in preparing for and responding to terrorist events and created a new discipline called "public health preparedness" that I would work in for the next 10 years. I was living in a time and place that would go down in history as world-changing.

When I discovered the German Chancellor Fellowship in 2002, there was a sincere concern that some foreign countries, like Iraq, could use disease as a weapon of mass destruction. The United States was undertaking unprecedented measures to prepare for a possible bioterrorism attack with smallpox, the world's only eradicated disease, by vaccinating thousands of hospital and healthcare workers. I was fascinated by the level of attention, money, and effort that was going into this measure. I wondered how a country like Germany, at the center of Europe with nine country borders, would address this same threat because a smallpox outbreak could cause a global pandemic. This curiosity led me to a unique and timely fellowship project idea.

For my application, I proposed developing a report on how Germany was preparing for bioterrorism and pandemic events and tied this project with the work I was doing at DOHMH in New York City. I felt this would be a timely and eye-catching project, unlike that of any other applicant. There was also a degree of urgency to this project because of the fear that foreign countries would use smallpox and other diseases as bioterrorism weapons in the near future.

A challenge to this application was identifying a "host" in Germany: a university or organization that would provide me with a desk space, resources, and a mentor to help open doors while I complete my project. I had to find this host during the application process, when I had no German language skills, no international contacts, and no promise I would win the award. I wasn't sure how to secure a host, so I just tried different tactics through trial and error. I researched organizations in Germany related to emergency management and sent cold emails, in English, introducing myself and requesting a phone meeting. Most of my emails were not responded to, but I was able to get in touch with and achieve a host through Dr. Wolf Dombrowsky at the University of Kiel's Disaster Research Center (with a hilariously long German name, the "Katastrophenforschungsstelle").

With this, my application was complete. It took me six months to carefully put this application together, and every day was needed; I couldn't have prepared well with less time. I wrote a personal statement and project proposal and requested and prepared my referees for three detailed recommendation letters. I was thrilled when I received the call that I was selected as a finalist for an interview.

When I arrived at the group interview event at the German Embassy in Washington, DC, I noticed many of the candidates were older and more credentialed. I didn't allow this to rattle me. In the interview, I continued to emphasize the timeliness and urgency of my project idea. This helped cinch my selection for the 2003 cohort of German Chancellor Fellows. I was selected over more experienced candidates and became one of the program's youngest Fellows.

This example shows how timeliness can be a major plus to your application when other factors, like your years of work experience or credentials, are lacking compared to other candidates. Whenever possible, create timely projects and ideas to propose in your applications.

Demonstrate Timeliness Through Urgency

Urgency is a form of timeliness. An application is urgent when you include a specific reason why you need the opportunity now, and not later. For many years, I have taught applicants the concept of incorporating an urgency factor into applications because it can help them edge out other top contenders. When a selection committee has two or more highly qualified candidates, they might lean toward the candidate who has a more urgent reason to be selected, as was the case in the story of June and Carmen at the beginning of this chapter.

A candidate who does not express urgency can still become a finalist, but a selection committee could reason that this candidate will be less negatively impacted by a rejection than another candidate with urgency and can responsibly encourage them to reapply next year or access other opportunities for their goals.

So, if you have a reason why your selection is urgent and should not be delayed, add it to your pitch! Some examples of situations that would warrant a mention of urgency include the following:

- **The opportunity is the only one offering the resources you need right now,** such as access to specific stakeholders, the opportunity to be in a specific location, or the opportunity to gain skills or resources needed for an immediate goal during or just after the opportunity.
- **You are researching a "fleeting phenomenon," something happening now but not later,** such as the recovery operation of a recent disaster, the immediate impact of new legislation, or the biography of a famous person facing a terminal illness.
- **Your work would contribute to a longer-term initiative already in progress,** such as conducting research to support a new program or draft a new policy, gaining specialized skills or expertise needed for a long-term project underway, or building a product with a near-future release date that capitalizes on a current market trend.

- **You would participate in a relevant, one-time event happening during the award period,** such as attending a conference, joining a gathering of experts in your field, or attending an exhibition, that won't recur in the future.

If your application to a competitive opportunity does not currently have an element of urgency, consider how you can incorporate one that will add value to your pitch and your long-term goals. Here are a few strategies:

- Read up on current events and brainstorm ways to tie the impact of those events to your proposal.
- Research conferences and events related to your topic happening during the funding award period that you can incorporate into your proposal.
- Identify new programs or initiatives in the idea, planning, or development stage that you could contribute to and consider ways in which your project could impact the outcome of an event, policy, or program happening in the near future.
- If you are applying for an opportunity that would prepare you for a goal in one or two years, such as entering graduate school, identify how the opportunity will give you skills and experiences that will make you more successful entering graduate school.

Case Study: Incorporating Urgency into Your Pitch   Camille Serrano, a first-generation college graduate, worked with me and ProFellow coach Rachel Santarsiero to ensure that she could apply her highest possible effort to her graduate school applications and graduate fellowships for funding. When she received eight acceptances from top master's programs in international affairs in the United States and abroad and reflected on what gave her an edge, she told me that urgency was one of the primary factors that she learned and applied from the MATCH ME Formula®.

In her winning 2024 application to the Master in International and Development Studies at the Geneva Graduate Institute, she emphasized her highly specific career goal and her desire to contribute to current crises occurring in the world at that time. She began her personal statement with a story of a timely crisis that influenced her career trajectory. She wrote:

> *In August 2021, the U.S. government announced it would withdraw armed forces from Afghanistan. News coverage depicted chaos, broadcasting images of Afghans clinging to departing American military planes at the Kabul airport, which motivated me to help Afghans in need. I quickly mobilized to work on the Afghan evacuation, laying the foundations of what would later become the Afghan Future Fund, a project at Rockefeller Philanthropy Advisors dedicated to supporting at-risk Afghans. It was during this time I discovered philanthropy's unique ability to respond to crises and informs my application to the Geneva Graduate Institute's Master in International and Development Studies program.... In collaboration with AFF, I have facilitated evacuation and resettlement support to over 4,800 Afghans across three continents. This experience taught me how to listen to partners and communities and develop tools to better serve them, and I aim to continue expanding this ability.*

Later in her essay, she tied these events to her future career goals and the urgency of needing new skills and expertise that could be achieved only through graduate study. In her statement, she wrote:

> *My ultimate goal is to work in an executive leadership position at a leading social justice foundation like the Ford Foundation to provide grant funding, technical assistance, and network building to communities across the globe and strive toward a more just world. Crises including the 2021 Afghanistan withdrawal, the 2022 Russian invasion of Ukraine, and the 2023 Hamas attack on Israel and humanitarian crisis in Gaza have reinforced my determination for a strong humanitarian response for those fleeing for safety and security.*

I am applying to the Graduate Institute's Master in International and Development Studies to deepen my understanding of the institutions and frameworks that shape humanitarian policy and hone leadership skills to expand philanthropy's ability to respond to humanitarian crises. The Graduate Institute's program will help me achieve my career goals because it offers specializations like Human Rights and Humanitarianism which can teach me how to anticipate socio-political and economic impacts to guide crisis response decisions through courses like "Predicting Crisis" with Professor Ravinder Bhavnani ...and "Managing and Solving Refugee Problems" with Professor Salvatore Lombardo.... Studying in Geneva will be crucial in shaping my future philanthropic leadership, especially in responding to crises that require cross-border collaboration and diverse expertise.... To meet the moment of complex crises now, I seek the analytical framework and methodological foundation offered by the Graduate Institute's program to enhance my understanding of the barriers communities face and equip me to use philanthropy as a more flexible tool for driving systemic change.

Camille's urgency is subtle, in words like "to meet the moment of complex crises now." You also feel urgency in the tone of her highly detailed statement, where she mentions key current events and several unique benefits of the graduate program that she would capitalize on to achieve her specific career goals and contribute to timely challenges. These touches of timeliness and urgency can make a huge difference in a competition where selectors are choosing between many highly qualified candidates. With all factors equal, they will preference candidates who are addressing timely challenges and have a more urgent reason to be selected now.

Some candidates get stuck on the idea of adding timeliness and urgency to their application because they sometimes feel there just isn't anything timely about their project idea and have no specific reason to undertake the opportunity now rather than later. But if you have applied these brainstorming strategies and still conclude there is no genuine timeliness or urgency to your application, I would challenge you to reflect on why. In some cases, it might be because the opportunity is misaligned with your personal mission and interests. Listen to those signals. I believe that if you deeply want the opportunity and are committed to putting in a high effort, you can always find creative ways to make your pitch both timely and urgent.

Key Takeaways

- One way to give yourself an edge in the competition is to express why your selection is timely and urgent. When faced with choosing among two or more equally qualified candidates, selectors may preference the candidate who addresses a timely issue and has a more urgent reason to be selected now and not later.
- Demonstrate timeliness by expressing how your ideas for contribution will address problems that are a priority for the organization now and in the immediate future.
- Demonstrate urgency by highlighting the benefits that would be sacrificed if you are not selected now.

Your Turn

Consider the opportunity you are targeting. Using what you have learned in this chapter, identify the organization's current challenges and goals and select one way you can contribute to one of their top priorities using your unique skills, expertise, and perspective from your lived experience. In addition, identify a reason why you need this opportunity now, and not later, to include in your pitch.

5 | Capitalize on the Organization's Unique Benefits

Turn Their Brag Points into Your Bonus Points

Craig Isakow is the only entrepreneur I know who was accepted to pitch on *Shark Tank* and was also accepted to the world's most well-known Silicon Valley business accelerator, Y Combinator. Craig happens to be married to a long-time friend, so I reached out to him to ask how he positioned himself for these two very competitive, but also very different, business investment opportunities. His story blew me away.

Craig is an entrepreneur who is unabashedly an expert at understanding what selectors need and finding a way to deliver on those needs. Early in his career, he used his pitch skills to become the only person in his graduating class at the University of Michigan to land a sought-after position at McKinsey. He was also later selected for the Wharton Business School, one of the most competitive MBA programs in the world. In the course of his career, Craig founded and grew several companies in a range of industries.

Craig has demonstrated his superpower of getting selected for highly competitive opportunities. For each opportunity he applied to, he expressed how he would capitalize on the opportunity's unique benefits.

Craig's extraordinary appearance on ABC's *Shark Tank* came first. *Shark Tank* is a popular reality TV show where business founders are filmed pitching their business for an investment to five "Sharks," including famous entrepreneurs like Mark Cuban, a technologist billionaire, and Lori Greiner of QVC fame. Because the show offers entrepreneurs immediate exposure to millions of viewers and the opportunity to get an investment from a celebrity Shark, nearly 40,000 founders apply to be on *Shark Tank* each season, but less than 100 ultimately appear on the show (John 2025).

In 2013, Craig had an idea for a computer webcam cover at a time when former intelligence contractor Edward Snowden was all over the news with conspiracy theories that the FBI was spying on Americans through their computer cameras. Craig hired a freelance MIT student to produce a prototype of the small plastic clip with a sliding cover using a 3D printer and named it Eyebloc. A plumber who came by Craig's house asked about the product spread out on Craig's kitchen table and suggested he apply to *Shark Tank*. Craig hadn't considered it before, but just two weeks earlier, he learned at a family wedding that his cousin's boyfriend was a former producer on *Shark Tank*. Taking it as a sign, he reached out to learn how he could get on the show.

The connection got him an opportunity to pitch the show's producer, and he was coached to lean in heavily on the conspiratorial "spy blocking" angle of his product, which would add an attractive element of drama to his pitch. Understanding that the producer's goal is to create great entertainment, he took the advice of his connection to act "crazier" while recording his video pitch for his *Shark Tank* application. Although he felt ridiculous yelling at the camera with eyes bulging, Craig kept ramping up the energy as he yelled, "America, you're being watched!" It worked. Before he had even sold one Eyebloc, he was invited to be one of the lucky few to film at the studio and be aired on an episode during the fifth season of the show.

Although Craig was thrilled to be selected for the show, he knew that his chance of getting a deal from a Shark was unpredictable because the show's primary mission is to create TV entertainment. Despite his preparation, Craig's pitch for $50,000 in exchange for 10% equity in his new Eyebloc company bombed. While some of the Sharks saw the need for the product (webcam blockers are now a household commodity), others laughed him off the floor, with one Shark calling his product "crap on a stick" (Authority Magazine 2020).

But was the *Shark Tank* rejection a complete failure for Craig? Not at all. Being selected for the show allowed him to capitalize on the show's unique benefit of getting his little-known company free, national TV coverage. The day the episode aired, Craig sold $80,000 worth of Eyebloc product. Craig also became part of a small, special network of *Shark Tank* participants that includes the founders of now well-known companies like Bombas, Ring, and Squatty Potty. His Eyebloc side hustle grew to several hundred thousand dollars in sales and was a key building block of his future Y Combinator pitch.

Craig learned a lot from the *Shark Tank* experience about how to hone his pitch for investment as he went on to found and have more success with his next companies. About eight years later, Craig and his co-founder Allan Fisch, representing their new start-up Moonshot Brands, were selected for the Winter 2021 cohort of Y Combinator.

Y Combinator (YC) is a globally competitive three-month program to help start-ups accelerate their revenue growth by providing unique resources and mentorship from business experts, as well as opportunities to raise money from venture capitalists before and during a widely publicized "Demo Day" (Y Combinator 2025). YC also invests $500,000 in every company for a small equity stake.

Getting into YC is no small feat. YC states that for each cohort, they receive more than 10,000 applications for approximately 125 spots, a 1% acceptance rate. The program is highly sought after because YC has an extraordinary track record of choosing and investing in more than 90 billion-dollar companies, including Stripe, Airbnb, and Reddit (Broe 2025).

For Craig, Y Combinator was an opportunity that had unique benefits similar to *Shark Tank*, including national exposure and access to investors, but a completely different mission and goals than the reality show. YC is fully focused on creating successful companies. Knowing that there was an extreme level of competition for YC, Craig did his research to identify a unique angle that would show how he would capitalize on the unique benefits YC offered.

Moonshot Brands was an e-commerce aggregator that acquired and grew profitable e-commerce companies by leveraging shared marketing and operational resources. This was not a completely unique idea, but at the time, it was new and trending; several other companies like his recently received investments from top venture capital firms. Craig noticed that Y Combinator did not yet have an e-commerce aggregator in their portfolio. He knew that venture capitalists like to follow trends in the investment space because, despite the hype, they are relatively risk-averse: their goal is to find and accelerate high-growth companies with business models that have traction in the market. This gave him an idea.

In their YC pitch, Craig and Allan discussed how they would be YC's first e-commerce aggregator and briefly mentioned competitor VC firms that had invested in similar companies. They also mentioned that they already had investors, including someone who was an early YC participant. This indicated to the selectors that they understood the unique benefits of the YC platform: the sought-after investor network. Craig and Allan were selected by showing how they would capitalize on the program's unique benefits, in addition to being memorable, timely, and aligned with YC's mission of creating a great investment opportunity.

Craig's applications demonstrate the *C* of the MATCH ME Formula®, which stands for *Capitalizes on the organization's unique benefits*. **Capitalize is an action word that represents how you will leverage the organization's unique benefits to help them achieve their mission and yours.**

In all applications, it's important to articulate what the opportunity's unique benefits are and how you will activate them to achieve a mutually beneficial outcome. This helps you achieve a compelling story "hook" that makes the selectors and the opportunity the "hero" of your application story.

In this chapter, you will learn:

- Why capitalizing on the organization's unique benefits matters
- How to find the organization's unique benefits
- Ways to capitalize on the organization's unique benefits
- How to make the organization the "hero" of your application story

Why Capitalizing on the Organization's Unique Benefits Matters

Whether you are applying for a selective job, a funding award, a competitive graduate school spot, or a business accelerator, selectors will inevitably ask: "Why are you applying to this opportunity?"

In most cases, selectors are seeking a response tailored to them, mentioning their unique benefits. This question is used to gauge not only your knowledge of the organization but also your authentic desire and enthusiasm for the opportunity. How you propose to capitalize on their unique benefits (or not) will demonstrate if you are a serious candidate (or not).

When you answer the question "Why are you applying to this opportunity?" with a response that is so general it could be applied to similar opportunities, you are sending the underlying message that you do not have a thoughtful idea of how you will leverage their unique benefits to achieve your goals or, worse, have no idea what their unique benefits are.

Even if you are a very strong candidate based on your record of accomplishments, a generic response to this question can signal that you are applying to lots of similar opportunities and you might not accept their offer. This happens when candidates use the same personal statement with only slight tweaks for several colleges or graduate programs or the same cover letter for lots of job applications. You may have received the feedback from a mentor that your personal statement or cover letter is strong, but if it's not tailored to each opportunity you apply to with a discussion of their unique benefits, it's weak. Whenever you skip the step of tailoring, you relinquish the chance to be considered a serious candidate.

When you research and mention their unique benefits, you help the selectors understand how serious you are about being selected for the opportunity, how your selection is mutually beneficial, and whether your gains from the opportunity are more significant for you than for other candidates. This strategy is especially effective when you discuss how you will leverage their unique benefits in new, innovative ways when combined with your expertise, network, and lived experience that other candidates don't offer. Like mission alignment and timeliness, this tactic helps candidates get selected over people who have strong résumés but do not mention the organization's unique benefits in their pitch.

So, as a first step, identify the unique benefits of the organization offering a sought-after opportunity. This research will also help you determine whether the benefits are so unique that you cannot access them anywhere else, making the opportunity invaluable to your goals.

How to Find the Organization's Unique Benefits

Every organization works hard to differentiate itself from its competitors that offer similar services and solutions. They make investments and carefully choose the right staff, focus areas, and resource offerings that help them achieve their mission and goals, giving them fodder to attract top talent and accomplishments to share in the press, on their website, and in their marketing materials.

The more closely you look at similar organizations, the more you will notice how different their organizations are in how they fulfill their mission. Here are some examples of organizations that have a similar mission but unique benefits that create different approaches and outcomes:

- **Nike and Adidas** are the top two sneaker companies globally, but they have different product styles and features, target audiences, headquarter locations, technological capabilities, advertising messages, leaders and employee teams, operational strategies, and workplace cultures, among other unique factors.
- **The Nature Conservancy and Greenpeace** are nonprofit organizations that both have a mission to support environmental conservation, but they have different focus areas, donors, leadership and staff, budget levels, political influence, monitoring approaches, and outcomes.
- **Harvard University and Stanford University** both offer a globally competitive Master in Business Administration, but each program has unique coursework, faculty, subfocus areas, research institutes, employer partnerships, career and business start-up resources, locations, and alumni networks.
- **Echoing Green and Ashoka Fellows** are similar fellowship programs that support social entrepreneurs, helping them to advance their reach, impact, and leadership acumen, but these fellowships have unique selection criteria, programming, mentors, funding awards, community engagement, and alumni networks.

- **Y Combinator and Tech Stars** are two of the most well-known business accelerators in the world that offer seed funding and mentorship to start-up entrepreneurs, but these accelerators have different focuses and philosophies, and they offer unique programming, mentorship styles, investor networks, locations, cohort sizes, and funding amounts.

The unique benefits of the opportunities you are applying for may not be obvious. Like mission research, you'll need to look for their unique benefits in primary and less obvious places. You can also use AI tools to identify differences among organizations, degree programs, accelerators, and awards. You'll want to look closely at how they differ from similar programs by their:

- Mission and goals
- Approaches to problems
- Focus areas
- Size, assets, and resources
- Leadership and staff
- Partnerships and stakeholders
- Influence, reputation, and political caché
- Budget, profits, and funding
- Locations
- Mentor and alumni networks
- Programming or course offerings

In the process of doing your mission research on the organization offering an opportunity, you can find and jot down the organization's unique benefits that you cannot find elsewhere. If you are unsure if a particular benefit they offer is unique, keep in mind—*they* will know! Pay close attention to what they brag about on their website, in the news, and during events.

Here are some key places where you can find an organization's brag points on what makes them different from their competitors:

- **Website and press releases:** Within the organization's website, check out the "About" and "FAQs" pages to learn about the unique history and operation of the organization; check out information on their products, services, programs, features, and other offerings; review leadership and staff who may be considered leaders in the broader industry based upon their speaking at conferences, publications, and features in industry and national media; and read recent press releases announcing new initiatives. The website will contain gold nuggets of information about their unique benefits that you can use to answer their question "Why us?"

- **Marketing materials:** A company, organization, or university's marketing materials are where brag points live because they use these materials to attract customers, partners, top talent, and media attention. What outcome, initiatives, features, and assets do they say are the best or unique among their competitors?

- **Partnerships:** Many organizations have partnerships to advance their mission, and a partnership among two or more independent bodies is a unique benefit to everyone involved. Identify the purpose of the partnership and how the partnership enhances the organization's work. You may be able to create an idea of how you would leverage a partnership for a greater impact if selected for the opportunity.

- **AI tools:** You can use a tool like ChatGPT to ask what makes an organization, program, or opportunity different from others, using two or more opportunities for comparison. For example, if you are researching master of public policy programs, you can ask an AI tool things like: *what are the primary differences between the*

University of Minnesota's Master of Public Policy and the University of Maryland's Master of Public Policy? If the response is not detailed enough, continue with more specific questions such as: *do the University of Minnesota's Master of Public Policy and the University of Maryland's Master of Public Policy have differences in career services and professional development resources for students?* Keep in mind that AI tools can hallucinate, so make sure you confirm that the information it generates is accurate on the program's websites.

These are just a few places where you can find the organization's unique benefits, but don't rely solely on the Internet! One of the most effective ways to find this information is through speaking with leaders, staff, and admissions representatives you meet at conferences, info sessions, and social events. Ask them: "What makes this program [or organization] different?"

Through conversations, you might strike gold and find out about a new asset, initiative, or partnership that is not yet shared online, and create an idea for how you will leverage this new benefit if you are selected. You can create the mirage of being "telepathic" about the organization's latest happenings, helping you to stand out among your competitors. You will be sending a strong underlying message that you are resourceful in building relationships and gathering information, which is a skill all organizations seek.

Ways to Capitalize on the Organization's Unique Benefits

People who stand out as top contenders are skilled at proposing creative ways to leverage the organization's unique benefits in new and innovative ways. Doing this well takes some experience and practice, because you must tie in your unique expertise, lived experience, skills, and industry knowledge to pose an idea that is entirely new.

For example, imagine you are applying for a leadership position at a company that is facing challenges like lost revenue or increased production costs that are negatively impacting its bottom line. From your past corporate experience partnering with the public sector on sustainability initiatives, you realize that the company is uniquely positioned to be eligible for a new federal grant to implement environmental sustainability measures because of its unique factors: they are women-owned and located in a region with an increased risk of natural disasters due to climate change. Because the grant is new and not well-known, you may be the first person to share this opportunity with them. This grant would not only help them operate more efficiently and save money, but it would also create positive public relations that could support sales. This can be an idea you share in your interview for the role. Even if this grant idea is ultimately not feasible, by proposing a new idea like this, you display your creativity, expertise, and resourcefulness, signaling that you are already thinking ahead about how you will contribute to their mission.

Actively look for ideas that you are uniquely qualified to execute at the organization to help you stand out. Your ideas do not need to be perfect; they just need to be thoughtful. If you have an idea that you want to share in an application or interview but you're worried it is not feasible or has been tried before, just say so! You can say, "Although I lack the internal details to know if this is feasible, I have an idea to . . ." or "This may have been tried before, but I recognize there's an opportunity to test . . . ."

If the selectors respond that it is not feasible or has been tried before, this is not a bad thing—you have initiated a conversation! Listen carefully to any feedback, which gives you information that other candidates may not have. You may be able to use that insider information to continue the conversation and pose an idea that is even better.

A great place to add more thought to the idea you posed in an interview is in your "thank you" email. In addition to thanking them for the opportunity to interview, share a new idea that was sparked by the conversation. I have done this after every important job interview I have undertaken, and I believe it made a difference in my selection. This extra effort helps you to stand out as a memorable candidate. Keep in mind, it's not the idea itself but your strategic thinking and proactiveness in developing ideas that create a lasting positive impression on the selectors.

 Tip: When interviewing for a dream role, add unique ideas on how you will contribute if you are selected to your post-interview "thank you" email to selectors.

When you share ideas on how you would capitalize on an organization's unique benefits and contribute to their goals in an interview, listen carefully for any feedback or inside information about the organization that could generate additional ideas. A great place to continue advocating for your selection is in your follow-up "thank you" email. If you realized after the conversation that you had a new idea for how you could contribute, mention it after thanking them for the opportunity to interview. This will help you stand out as a candidate and help you stick in the mind of the selectors long after your interview.

© Pitch Your Potential / Vicki Johnson, Ph.D.

Years ago I interviewed for a policy position at the San Francisco Public Utilities Commission (PUC). In the interview, I learned a lot about what the PUC did and how it operated by asking in-depth questions. In the interview, my future boss asked how I would approach the first 90 days of the job. I gave a response, but after the interview, I worried I didn't give enough specific ideas, which would have been an important opportunity to show how I would capitalize on the organization's unique benefits and assets. So I took the matter into my own hands, sending her this follow-up email the next business day:

Subject: Thinking ahead: my first 90 days

Dear [name],

I hope you had a wonderful weekend. I appreciated the opportunity to meet with you on Friday and I wanted to summarize for you some ideas for how I would approach the position if given the opportunity.

My first priority would be to get up to speed on the current policy issues. As expected, I would review all relevant documents and agendas, and set up brief phone/in-person meetings with the Policy Analysts, lobbyists, and the PUC's subject matter experts to get an overview of their projects and policy areas. I would also ensure I understand the internal and external communication protocols.

I would then learn about and begin scoping the PUC's current policy capacities and relationships. I would develop an understanding of the PUC's working relationship with Senator Feinstein's office and others and the policy agendas. I would develop a strong working knowledge of the PUC's policy positions and identify areas that are in need of or may benefit from original research, literature reviews, or stakeholder input.

I would also scope the PUC's representation on state and national associations and advocacy coalitions. I would identify the groups that are the most politically influential, develop a system for tracking the PUC's input to these groups (if a system does not already exist), and identify subcommittees and projects that may need representation. I would develop a strategy to ensure the PUC's liaisons are participating effectively and determine if we have the right representation.

I would also develop a plan for cultivating new, long-term relationships with state and federal legislators. Perhaps working collaboratively with the Policy Analysts, I would research federal and state legislators who are working on issues of interest to the PUC, develop a short list of potential strategic partnerships, and develop an outreach plan with specific benchmarks. For example, the outreach plan may suggest partnering with other major municipal or state utilities to develop briefing materials for key issues or request a legislative hearing.

Of course, this would be in addition to ongoing projects and reactive work. I would have a much better sense of where I can help fill in the gaps once in the position, but I wanted to let you know I am thinking ahead.

Thank you again for your consideration.

This was a long email, but I put the full body of the email here to help you understand the level of detail I applied. There was no immediate response, but three days later, I was offered the position!

Make the Organization the "Hero" of Your Application Story

The ideal way to make the selectors the "hero" in your application story is to propose specific ideas of how you will capitalize on the organization's unique benefits if you are selected and create an outcome that is mutually beneficial: helping you achieve your personal mission and helping them achieve their organizational mission. **The most effective application story "hook" demonstrates that without the one-of-a-kind benefits the organization offers, your goal may not be achieved.** Consequently, you should mention the benefits that cannot be accessed elsewhere and why this opportunity is the ideal, if not only, opportunity to achieve your highly specific goal.

This approach does not work if you mischaracterize who the "hero" is. Some candidates make themselves the "hero" of the story, couching themselves as the person who will save them from their challenges or make them look good. Instead of detailing how they will capitalize on the organization's unique benefits to create a mutually beneficial outcome, these candidates detail their background and accomplishments to express why they are the "perfect" candidate. You might assume this approach would work, given that the selectors primarily ask questions about you, but it usually has the opposite effect. When you act as if you are the "hero," even unintentionally, you are sending the message that you believe they need you more than you need them, and give the impression that you lack a growth mindset and won't be a team player.

On the other hand, making the organization the "hero" of your application story and expressing why you want to access their unique benefits is *not* begging them to select you based on your needs. Most opportunities outside of undergraduate scholarships are merit-based, not needs-based, even if they help you meet a financial need. A needy ask can also have a negative effect on your candidacy because this tone devalues what you offer and gives the sense that you have a lot more to gain than they do if they select you.

Remember: organizations are seeking people who are in the best position to help them advance their organizational mission. Making them the "hero" means treating the opportunity as an ideal collaboration to advance their mission and your personal mission, while still honoring that they are deciding whether you will be selected over other qualified candidates. Making them the "hero" of your application story is a matter of respect!

So, express respect by providing specific ideas on how you will capitalize on their unique benefits when they ask you: "Why are you applying to this opportunity?" This emphasizes your mission alignment while also giving you an opportunity to highlight the skills, expertise, and unique lived experiences that you would bring to the role.

As an example of how this works in real life, consider a typical graduate school application. Most graduate schools ask applicants to address in their personal statement the question: "Why are you applying to this program?" Graduate school selectors are aware that most applicants are applying to several schools at once. Your response to this question helps the selectors gauge if you have an authentic desire to attend their program and if you will leverage everything the school has to offer.

In any graduate admissions cycle, top graduate schools always have more qualified applicants than they have spots on offer. It's a mistake to give a response to the question "Why are you applying to this program?" that is so generic that it could be applied to any other graduate program. They can't tell from a generic response if they are your top-choice school (even if you say this explicitly). Especially if you are a strong candidate, the selectors want to know if their program ranks highly for you compared to other programs.

If you name at least two to three of the school's unique benefits that would help you achieve your future goals, selectors will receive the underlying message that you are a serious candidate who is likely to accept their offer. On the other hand, if you couch their benefits broadly—for example, saying you appreciate "the esteemed faculty" rather than naming one or two specific faculty members—you'll give the message that you are not a serious candidate because you don't know what makes their program unique.

So, while you might believe it is a smart, time-saving shortcut to use the same personal statement for every school and just change the name of the school within, your lack of tailored responses may become the primary reason you face rejections as a highly qualified candidate.

Offer declines from candidates are a particular concern for universities that have a high ranking because their ranking can be negatively impacted by a low "yield rate": the percentage of accepted students who ultimately enroll. Universities want the percentage of their chosen applicants who accept the offer to be as high as possible, which means they won't make an offer to someone who is unlikely to accept, no matter how strong their application.

Likewise, offer declines are a major concern for companies recruiting for management and leadership roles, as well as fellowships and awards, that have a monthslong recruitment process. After spending an enormous amount of time and resources reviewing, interviewing, and selecting a candidate, they don't want their offer to be declined. If you give any indication during the selection process that you are not that serious and might decline their offer, especially by being vague about why you are applying to the opportunity, you are less likely to be selected, no matter how strong your résumé is.

Make every opportunity you apply to "the one"—your perfect match. This is easier to do when you apply only to opportunities for which you have an authentic desire and are fully aligned with your personal mission.

Case Studies: Capitalizing on the Organization's Unique Benefits I have worked with many graduate school and fellowship candidates who developed the skill of capitalizing on the program's unique benefits to stand out and get selected for highly competitive awards. The first example here is an excerpt from Jack Sullivan's statement of purpose (SoP) for his successful acceptance to the Ph.D. in Statistics and Operations Research (STOR) at the University of North Carolina—Chapel Hill (UNC). In 2023, the UNC STOR Ph.D. program had a 5% acceptance rate. Jack also successfully received acceptances and full funding offers from two other universities.

Note the level of specificity he used to answer the SoP prompt: "Your statement should reflect your professional goals, as well as familiarity with the program and faculty at UNC-Chapel Hill."

He wrote:

> *UNC's STOR Ph.D. program will allow me to develop the theoretical understanding and interdisciplinary skillset to achieve my goal through its coursework and research opportunities. At UNC, I will have the unique opportunity to study probability theory and optimization while*

staying within the core department so that I can develop the theoretical understanding needed to research the limitations of data-driven decision-making... Three faculty of particular interest are Dr. Amarjit Budhiraja, Dr. Yao Li, and Dr. Michael O'Neil. With Dr. Budhiraja, I could make data-driven decision-making fairer and more resilient by studying the impact of large deviations and rare events. This work can decrease the harm a rare event will cause and enable more widespread adoption of data-driven decision-making. The perspective on societal systems I learned through my degree in Politics and Philosophy will help identify societal implications and new directions. With Dr. Li, I could achieve my goal of making data-driven decision-making more resilient by making machine learning and statistical models robust against adversarial examples. Understanding which machine learning models respond best to adversarial examples will help define their practical limitations. With Dr. O'Neil, I could work to advance the theory of continuous nonlinear optimization methods. Increasing the theoretical understanding of these methods will increase their accountability. Additionally, Dr. O'Neil and I have a shared interest in federated learning. I would like to explore the synergies between my work on Approximate FedSplit and his work on FedHM. Learning to perform research at UNC will enable me to make data-driven decision-making more resilient, fair, and accountable.

In this excerpt you'll notice several unique benefits Jack highlighted, including "the unique opportunity to study probability theory and optimization" and the specific parallels between his research interests and the research areas of three named faculty. Jack's SoP is a good example of the level of detail and specificity needed for any highly competitive application process.

The following is an excerpt of a personal statement by an applicant named Bethany (not her real name) for her successful application for a juris doctorate at the University of Minnesota Law School, where she also received a significant merit-based scholarship. This statement also mentions several of the law school's unique benefits, including specific faculty, helping make it a standout application. Her application prompt stated: "An applicant's personal statement should explain why he or she wishes to obtain a law degree at the University of Minnesota."

In her personal statement, she wrote:

I am interested in the University of Minnesota because it will enable me to explore my known interests related to racial justice, neurolaw, and international human rights law. For example, through speaking with former terrorists for my master's research . . . I became interested in the path that leads to terrorism or criminality. While my master's degree gave me insight into the social and cultural components that contribute to the creation of that mindset, it also showed me the limitations of that approach. As home to the Shen NeuroLaw Lab, the research conducted there by Dr. Shen offers a fascinating new way to understand the mindset of criminality and terrorism. The University of Minnesota is also home to a number of experts on conflict and security as part of its renowned Human Rights Center. One such expert I'd love to work with is Professor Fionnuala Ní Aoláin. In the course of my research throughout Northern Ireland, I developed an interest in the balance of protecting human rights while also preventing terrorism. For example, photographing the National Museum of Ulster's exhibit on the Troubles for my dissertation, I watched a teenager drag her friend over to a panel, point and say, "See! They still blame us." While preserving cultural heritage was recognized as a human right, so too was it understood to be potentially problematic in keeping hate and division alive. I would love to be part of Professor Aoláin's research team to contribute to scholarship protecting and advancing human rights throughout the world, especially in places working to create and preserve peace.

Mentioning the opportunity's unique benefits and how you will capitalize on them is the best way to replace "fluff" and repetitive ideas from your application with detailed sentences that are memorable, show alignment, and provide ideas that are timely and urgent. This is also the place where being highly specific is important, a factor of the MATCH ME Formula® that I will discuss in more detail in Chapter 6.

 Tip: Tailor your university personal statements to make each school feel like they are your top choice.

To create an effective personal statement that is memorable and shows your enthusiasm for the opportunity, discuss how you will capitalize on two or three of the unique benefits that no other school offers. You could mention how you would leverage specific research groups and institutes at the university, use named libraries or archives, join specific student organizations in your discipline, or access the university's local partnerships with specific organizations for volunteer opportunities and internships. Discuss how these one-of-a-kind resources are the key ingredients you need to achieve your highly specific career goal and future contribution to your field. This approach gives you bonus points over candidates who have better grades, test scores, and accomplishments but show a lack of authentic desire with their vague and generic responses.

© Pitch Your Potential / Vicki Johnson, Ph.D.

Key Takeaways

- *Capitalize* is an action word that represents how you will leverage the organization's unique benefits to help them achieve their mission and yours.
- In all applications, it's important to articulate what the opportunity's unique benefits are and how you will activate them to achieve a mutually beneficial outcome. This helps you achieve a compelling story "hook" that makes the selectors and the opportunity the "hero" of your application story.
- To find their unique benefits and brag points—the things that distinguish them from similar programs and competitors—research the organization's website, press releases, marketing materials, and partnerships. You can also use AI tools like ChatGPT to find comparative differences. Also speak with leaders, staff, and admissions representatives for their input on what makes the organization different.
- To make the selectors the "hero" in your story, propose specific ideas of how you will capitalize on the organization's unique benefits if you are selected and create an outcome that is mutually beneficial: helping you achieve your personal mission and helping them achieve their organizational mission.
- The most effective application story "hook" demonstrates that without the one-of-a-kind benefits the organization offers, your goal may not be achieved.
- People who stand out as top contenders are skilled at proposing creative ways to leverage the organization's unique benefits in new and innovative ways.

Your Turn

Using the selective opportunity you are targeting, research the organization and the opportunity itself to identify how they are different from similar organizations and opportunities. Find the organization's unique benefits from the following:

- Mission and goals
- Approaches to problems
- Focus areas
- Size, assets, and resources
- Leadership and staff
- Partnerships and stakeholders
- Influence, reputation, and political caché
- Budget, profits, and funding
- Locations
- Mentor and alumni networks
- Programming or course offerings

6 | Be **Highly Specific**

Use Detail That Captivates Selectors

When I walked into my first interview for my dream job at the age of 30, I was nervous. I was vying to become the policy director of the National Commission on Children and Disasters, a high-level leadership role. To say that I was less qualified than the other candidates is an understatement.

The commission was a new organization created by Congress to prepare an in-depth report for the Obama Administration with recommendations on how the United States should address the needs of children in disaster preparedness, response, and recovery. Stemming from the disastrous federal response to Hurricane Katrina, the commission's report had to address 11 distinct areas of impact on children, including education, childcare, physical and mental healthcare, emergency medical response, and emergency sheltering. The policy director role was a high-profile role that would involve coordinating and synthesizing the input of the 10 expert commissioners, all hand-selected leaders; Congressional and White House staff; leaders at federal, state, and local agencies; and practitioners.

At the time the policy director position opened, there was no question that I was deeply aligned with the mission of the commission. I had been working in the field of emergency management and public health since the World Trade Center attacks of 2001 and pursued roles, as well as professional fellowships, where I worked with stakeholders and performed research to inform policymakers. But I was young and looked even younger. My highest professional title was "Senior Analyst" at a professional association. The question would be whether I had what it would take to lead.

I learned about the job through a colleague, Stephanie Bardack, who sat near me at the Department of Health and Human Services (HHS) and noticed I was withering in an HHS contract role after being there for just two months. For the first several weeks in this new job, I was ready to dive into important work, but I had no clear title or direction on what I should be doing. So I identified a task that needed to be done and volunteered to create a remote work contingency plan for the agency's 40,000 employees in case of a pandemic (this was 2009, about a decade before the pandemic we all remember). But no one seemed to care that I was working on it, and Stephanie noticed my frustration.

One day, Stephanie came by my desk and said to me, "Vicki, some people I know are hiring a policy director for a new congressional commission on children and disasters. You've got emergency management policy experience—you should apply." She handed me the job description.

The first thing I noticed was that this policy director role was a temporary, two-year position, which was a downside for me. I was hoping my current contract position at HHS would lead to a permanent federal job, and I told her so. She looked at me in disbelief.

"Vicki, this is a killer job. *Everyone* wants to work for a commission. Think about the level of people you would get to meet and work with," she said. "You should apply."

She was right. My short-sighted view of the position completely changed.

I gave Stephanie my tailored résumé and cover letter and asked if she would refer me directly to the commission's new executive director, which she kindly did. That referral got me an interview. But I started to experience self-doubt. I heard through the grapevine that some others who landed interviews for the role had a lot more congressional experience, including one candidate with a doctorate and another with experience as a former executive director of a well-known DC nonprofit.

At this stage in my career, I had applied the MATCH ME Formula® elements successfully to land fellowships, jobs, and top graduate school acceptances, but this job application felt particularly high-stakes. The more I learned about the job, the more I wanted it, badly. The job responsibilities were those I loved doing, including research and writing, stakeholder engagement, policy analysis, and problem solving. I was also fascinated by the topic of children and disasters and excited about the prospects of gaining expertise in new areas of emergency management.

I decided to lean in on the approach of being highly specific and to express, with as much detail as possible, how I could help the small team achieve their two-year goal of creating a high-quality report of recommendations for Congress. I knew the commission's executive director did not come from an emergency management background, so I could offer expertise there. Also, having previously worked at the National Association of County and City Health Officials, which represents local health departments in policymaking at the national level, I knew that the commission would be best served by gathering existing policy recommendations from the many stakeholder groups based in Washington. My theory was that their buy-in to the development of the report would be key to the commission's success.

I wasn't sure if the executive director at the commission was thinking that far ahead yet or if he already had a completely different idea of how to approach the report, but I figured if I could lay out what a stakeholder engagement process would look like with my leadership, I would stand out from candidates who didn't offer a plan. It would also show how enthusiastic I was to be selected for the role.

I prepared intensively by developing a five-page strategic plan outlining, with clear subheadings and bullets, exactly how I would design, execute, and lead a broad stakeholder engagement process and the preparation of the final report by the two-year deadline. I mentioned specific groups and people I would tap, identified conferences and events that could be instrumental, and shared examples of my policy analysis from previous roles. During the first of what would be several interviews, I came with a printout of the plan. This physical document was going to be my "Hail Mary" once the executive director realized how young and inexperienced I was compared to my competitors.

It made an impression. They kept bringing me in for more interviews. During the entire application and interview process, I leaned heavily on being highly specific about what I would contribute. Knowing the political landscape in Washington, I also mentioned potential roadblocks the commission would be up against and how we could overcome them. Even if the ideas I proposed were not perfect, I believe bringing those detailed ideas to my interviews instilled confidence in my selectors that I had the expertise, poise, and organizational skills to succeed in the role. This approach got me the job!

Two years later when I asked the executive director why I was selected over other candidates for the role, he said simply, "You made a convincing case." My convincing case was not credentials or years of work experience; it was my highly specific plan for how I would get the job done. My detailed vision of the future was the primary reason I was able to land the role and beat out much more experienced candidates.

My experience applying for this job exemplifies the letter *H* in the MATCH ME Formula®, which stands for *Highly specific*. **Being highly specific, using memorable and effective detail, is a key aspect of every successful pitch for a dream job, award, or elite opportunity.**

In the course of leading ProFellow, I have interviewed hundreds of leaders, graduates of top universities, and multi-fellowship winners and asked what made their applications stand out. The most common theme was specificity, including being specific when describing career and impact goals and proposing niche, highly focused ideas for research, projects, and business initiatives.

To be a top contender for the world's most competitive opportunities, you must learn how to remove "fluff" and jargon from your pitch and replace it with clear, compelling details about your background, goals, and ideas. The organization and layout of these details are also important so that selectors can understand your ideas and assess if you have what it takes to be successful.

In this chapter, you will learn:

- Why specificity and detail matter
- How to recognize and eliminate platitudes and jargon in your writing
- How to create a highly specific MATCH ME Formula® career goal
- How to propose a highly specific project
- Tactics for obtaining highly specific recommendation letters

Why Specificity and Detail Matter

We value something that's one-of-a-kind over something that is common or mass-produced because it's special. You make your application special by including specific, highly curated details in every aspect of your pitch, including within your memorable anecdotes, your career highlights and skills, the ideas you propose, and the specific reasons why you are applying. You also get attention when you discuss a highly specific problem that you want to help solve. Selectors know that the skill of using high detail takes creativity, expertise, and vision.

I learned the power of being highly specific from my mom early in my life. Although my mom had limited resources to purchase decor, she had a defined vision and eye for her decorating style, which I would describe as Victorian-era country elegance. Our home displayed family heirlooms and wall art, feminine curtains and stenciling, and layered textures in throw pillows, patterned china, and handmade patchwork quilts. There were many vintage items and furniture made from distressed wood and weathered metals that she carefully selected from thrift stores and antique shops. My dad helped complete her vision by hand-renovating our small rowhouse to include exposed brick walls in our kitchen and a refinished antique mantelpiece in our living room.

When I was a teenager, I started to notice that my home was different from my friends' homes because it was more organized and detailed than most. Most of my friends' homes held a collection of well-loved furniture and personal things, but without any particular theme. Some friends' homes had a more polished look that mirrored a favorite department store but lacked originality.

As I grew older, I began to appreciate the detail in my mom's selection of colors, textures, and groupings to create beautiful interior designs, and I noticed that other people did as well. At age 43, she pursued and earned her bachelor's degree in art history, receiving the distinction of *magna cum laude*. She went on to work in boutiques and museums, including Winterthur, a historic DuPont mansion, where she had the chance to apply her skills and eye for design professionally.

From my mom's example, I learned that curation is a powerful art form. You can gain positive attention and become memorable when you create something that has high detail, especially when your creations demonstrate that you are paying attention to the desires of your audience. Think of a fancy restaurant or a beautiful wedding you attended. What you notice and enjoy are the small, curated details.

Creating an application that is highly specific, paying attention to the needs and interests of selectors, doesn't require any special resources. It just requires time, creativity, and the practiced skill of curation.

The biggest challenge to using high detail is the limited space you are given to express yourself. Cover letters and personal statements are typically expected to be limited to one page. Pitch decks, project proposals, and introductions are also expected to be succinct and to the point. To develop the skill of becoming more specific and detailed in a small space, you first need to unlearn the common use of platitudes and jargon.

Replace Platitudes and Jargon

Because most application documents have a space or word limit, we tend to use nonspecific language, like platitudes and jargon, often without realizing it. A *platitude* is a remark, usually with an idealist bent, that is vague and used too often to be interesting or helpful. Have you ever heard the platitude "I want to change the world"? Less used now, this phrase was at its height when I was in college. People would say or write this to express that they wanted to do something big and idealistic. It was used in commercials, books, and motivational speeches. The phrase went out of vogue because it is so cliché. But it has been replaced by other types of platitudes that are equally unhelpful, like "I want to make a social impact."

Because many people mistakenly believe job, school, and award competitions are a numbers game, they often spend all their precious word count detailing past accomplishments and use vague platitudes to describe their future goals. But I can tell you with certainty that this is the wrong approach. I often need to redirect candidates to remove details about their past (which are available in an accompanying résumé or CV) in order to add more detail about their future goals.

The words you select matter. We tend to use jargon in applications, proposals, and interviews because it's what we're used to hearing in commercial advertising, presentations, websites, and academic articles. *Jargon* is special words, phrases, and expressions that are used within a profession or group that are difficult for those outside those groups to understand. Jargon is the culprit of long sentences that are meant to sound powerful but are weak in achieving their goal.

Here are some examples of jargon in different sectors:

- **Academia:** *Prompting interdisciplinary, intersectional inquiry . . .*
- **Corporations:** *Enacting digitally-enabled transformation . . .*
- **Government:** *Operationalize policy frameworks for strategic alignment . . .*
- **Nonprofits:** *Implement evidence-based interventions at scale . . .*

What they really mean:

- **Academia:** *Using research that incorporates knowledge from different disciplines . . .*
- **Corporations:** *Using technology, we will change . . .*
- **Government:** *Aligning the goals of policymakers and constituents . . .*
- **Nonprofits:** *Once pilot programs are found to be effective, we test them with larger groups of people . . .*

An application full of jargon and platitudes leaves the reader with more questions than answers. It increases the risk that you'll be rejected because the selectors are confused by your pitch or must make assumptions to fill the gaps in information. When you break down jargon to simple words and when you replace platitudes with more specific language, your pitch will be easier to consume and understand, which will increase your chance of success.

> **Tip: If a 10-year-old can't understand it, it's probably jargon.**
>
> You never know who is reading your application or pitch. If they can't understand you, it's unlikely you or your ideas will be selected. Always try to replace jargon with succinct, easy-to-understand phrases that can be understood by a general audience.
>
> © Pitch Your Potential / Vicki Johnson, Ph.D.

Adding Words for Greater Specificity

Cover letters, personal statements, proposals, and pitches are *tactical* documents, not creative or academic writing. The goal of these written pieces is to explain "why you, why this opportunity, and why now" in a clear, concise manner. Except for awards acknowledging a past achievement, virtually all competitive opportunities are created for future impact. While you need to demonstrate that you can be successful using examples from your past accomplishments, the future-facing information about your vision and what you hope to achieve is more important than the past.

In place of platitudes and jargon, add detailed responses to the questions you're asked using simple words. Here are a few examples:

> **Vague:** *I help companies build their brand to achieve their strategic revenue goals.*
> **Specific:** *I help companies achieve a 2:1 return on investment in paid advertising by leveraging user-generated content, improving retargeting ads, and refining audience targeting.*

> **Vague:** *My goal is to help marginalized communities access the tools to build intergenerational wealth so they can have a brighter future for themselves and their families.*
> **Specific:** *My goal is to help first-generation immigrants access checking and savings accounts, financial literacy courses, and entrepreneurship capital such as Small Business Administration (SBA) loans, so that they can build wealth and save for health expenses, college education, and retirement.*

In reading how the vague sentences compare to the specific sentences, which ones sound better to you? Naturally, you can feel the strength of the sentences with added detail. Without knowing anything about the candidates who wrote these sentences, you will find yourself more compelled by the candidate with a specific idea of what they want to do in the future and how they will do it.

Removing Words for Greater Specificity

Adding more words does not necessarily make something more specific and detailed in a way that is helpful. Sometimes, removing words and replacing jargon with commonly used language is the best way to make your pitch highly specific.

For example, take this line from Accenture's "What We Do—Capabilities" web page (2025) to describe their customer service capabilities. They say:

> *Impersonal and inconsistent interactions are leaving organizations scrambling to understand how to better support customers. Delivering seamless, data-driven experiences that feel intuitive, not reactive, is vital to unlocking new opportunities for growth.*

What does that even mean?!

Personally, I would change this to:

> *We use data to identify and create better customer service experiences that increase your revenue.*

Companies and organizations can get away with using jargon, but this tactic will not serve you well in a competitive application. Review your writing to identify where you can remove words and phrases that are overly complex or redundant so you can create a sentence that is clear and specific. This not only helps the selectors better understand you but is a great way to free up word count so you have more space to add detail in other areas of your pitch.

Tip: To become a better interviewer and negotiator, practice writing without AI.

I mastered the skill of adding specificity to a single sentence quickly and easily through extensive writing practice, long before the advent of AI tools. I recommend you start to master this skill too, without the crutch of AI, so you can be someone who can speak with specificity on the spot in introductions, interviews, and negotiations.

© Pitch Your Potential / Vicki Johnson, Ph.D.

Create a Highly Specific Career Goal

The most common thing you'll be asked in the competitive application process for jobs, graduate schools, and leadership opportunities is: "What is your career goal?" Responses are often vague because the applicant doesn't have a specific career goal, or they do but believe it's better to express a general goal rather than a specific one. Some candidates also miss the intention of the question by responding that the opportunity itself is the career goal. What selectors are trying to assess with this question is whether you need the opportunity now and how you will make the most of it toward creating future impact that they care about.

You will be more memorable and more compelling as a candidate when you express a career goal that is extremely specific. A highly specific career goal helps the reader visualize the future you and more easily understand why you need the opportunity now to achieve that goal. It instills confidence that you know exactly what you want to do in the future and are intentionally pursuing the steps to get there. A highly specific and aspirational goal also signals that you are a high achiever. A vague goal or no goal signals you're an average performer who is not thinking ahead (even if that's not the case!).

The MATCH ME Career Goal

There are four components to a highly specific career goal, what I call a "MATCH ME Career Goal." They include:

- A specific type of role or position title
- At a specific type of organization (with a well-known example organization, if possible)
- Focused on a specific group you want to support or a specific problem you want to help solve
- With a tangible outcome

The purpose of being this specific is to help the reader visualize the future you in their mind as they read your statement, creating "stickiness" and connection with your selectors.

I've worked with many candidates, helping them take a vague career goal and transform it into something highly specific and aligned with the organization's mission. One example is from a master's student in economics, Damian, who was applying for a one-year research fellowship at a policy think tank that researches the impact of economic trends and policies on the U.S. economy. Damian did his mission research and found that the think tank's goal is to inform congressional policymakers with research that helps them make better policy decisions.

The application asked for a cover letter that would describe the applicant's background, long-term career goals, and motivations for applying to the fellowship. That's a lot to cover, so at first, Damian kept his career goal brief and added a lot of detail about his academic background and skills.

> **Damian's Original Career Goal:** *My career goal is to pursue a Ph.D. in business.*

To improve his cover letter, I encouraged Damian to reduce the details about his background in the cover letter, which are detailed in his CV, and demonstrate alignment with the organization's mission by crafting a much more specific career goal. He added his dream graduate program, a specific outcome, and a tangible social impact aligned with the organization's mission. Damian also added a line about how the fellowship opportunity was uniquely positioned to help him achieve this long-term goal, to create an application story "hook."

> **Damian's MATCH ME Career Goal:** *My career goal is to pursue a Ph.D. in Business at Rice University, which has a unique doctoral program in Strategic Management. I want to pursue scholarly research on effective business models of start-up companies developing new renewable energy technologies that need a capital investment of more than $10 million. The goal of this research would be to identify ways to increase public investment in green energy companies to help them undertake risky but necessary R&D and ultimately reduce the U.S. dependence on fossil fuels. As a Fellow at the Economic Policy Institute, I can begin the foundational work for this future dissertation research by gaining experience working with large data sets, connecting with academics and key stakeholders in the field, and identifying potential case studies.*

You'll notice Damian's original career goal might seem specific, but compared to the improved career goal, it lacked a lot of detail. The added detail improves the career goal statement in several ways:

- You can now visualize Damian in the future, working on a Ph.D. at Rice University, making the application story more memorable.
- You have a clear idea of Damian's personal mission for social impact.
- The detail provides a strong underlying message that Damian cares about finding solutions to address the U.S. dependence on fossil fuels through research.
- This career goal is highly aligned with the think tank's mission to create research on economic trends and policies that impact the U.S. economy.
- In the final line, you can see how Damian will capitalize on the organization's unique benefits, and why it is timely and urgent for him to undertake this fellowship now and not later.

Damian's career goal example provides an outline that works well for time-limited opportunities like internships, graduate programs, fellowships, and business accelerators. But, when applying for a permanent job, your future career goal should not give the impression that you might leave the organization within a year or two for a job elsewhere or for graduate study. Your career goal should be one that could be achieved within the organization. This not only helps the selectors see the future you but also sends the signal that you are prepared to make a long-term commitment to the organization.

This next career goal example is from a late-20s professional, Mei, who was applying to a program director position at a nonprofit organization that gives crowd-funded loans to small businesses in Africa and South America. The organization's mission is to create more opportunities and economic stability in these regions, with a special focus on women's empowerment.

Mei was invited to an interview after submitting a résumé and cover letter and receiving a referral through someone who previously worked at the organization. She prepared for the interview by undertaking a mock interview with me.

I started her mock interview with the question: "What are your career goals?"

> **Mei's Original Career Goal:** *My goal is to become a program director in your organization to apply my experience and skills in fundraising and program management and also develop expertise on how to engage local stakeholders in your portfolio countries in the Global South.*

When you first read this, you might think, "That sounds great and very specific!" But what this statement lacks is a clear picture of what Mei wants to do in the future because it is focused on the present day.

When I gave her this feedback, I encouraged Mei to imagine herself five years in the future at the same organization. If she stayed and was successful, what would she be doing? I encouraged her to make it a MATCH ME Career Goal. She tried again:

> **Mei's MATCH ME Career Goal:** *If I had the opportunity to work as a program director and was successful in increasing the number of small women-owned businesses receiving loan support, my future goal in a few years would be to move into a position as a regional director. In the near term, I'm particularly interested in contributing ideas to make the program more financially efficient, which would prepare me for a greater leadership role managing region-wide operations.*

Mei's original career goal stopped at the immediate opportunity, but her improved career goal paints a long-term vision of Mei's role at the organization. Its underlying meaning is that she is thinking ahead and will work hard to move up in the organization. The details about the outcomes she hopes to achieve show she understands and is highly aligned with their mission.

When you write out your career goal, you can assess if it is highly specific by asking yourself if it answers these questions:

- In what job role exactly, at what level?
- In what type of organization—corporate, government, non-profit, or academic? Or would you be an independent founder or scholar?
- Focused on which specific group of people?
- In what specific area of focus (if it's a broad field with many components)?
- To what specific and tangible outcome?

These questions will help you get closer to a defined and aspirational goal that will inspire selection committees.

 Tip: Projects are not career goals.

Make sure to include a specific job position and organization type for your career goal. For example, "develop a program to help single mothers start businesses" is a project, not a career goal. Make the project your specific outcome, and describe the role you want to play in executing this project, for example: *My career goal is to found an organization in the greater Chicago area that offers programs to help single mothers start businesses.*

© Pitch Your Potential / Vicki Johnson, Ph.D.

When You Don't Have a Specific Career Goal

You may get stuck on the exercise of improving your career goal statement to something highly specific because you have many interests and possible career paths. You might also worry you will get in trouble if you don't pursue the career goal you stated in your application in the future.

If you have many interests and possible career paths, just keep in mind that most people do not have a career goal that is as specific as the ones suggested here. The purpose of creating a highly specific career goal for your application is to help the selectors visualize you as a future leader. This exercise forces you to stretch your imagination further than you have before and put down on paper who you will be. Don't be afraid to dream big and get uncomfortable with the scale of your aspirations. Selectors are drawn to people who have high goals!

Defining a specific, aspirational career goal in an application does not set the goal in stone. The intention is to create a compelling application story using just one authentic career goal out of the tens of possible paths you might pursue. You may later do something different than what you state in your application, but this doesn't matter—there is no career goal police who will hold you accountable to what you wrote years before! Your highly specific career goal is simply a clear and compelling North Star that the rest of your pitch is built around.

That said, don't state a career goal that you would never actually pursue just to achieve an opportunity, because this means you are pursuing opportunities you don't authentically desire or that are a poor fit for the next stage in your career. You may think it is helpful to tell selectors what they want to hear, but if you find yourself writing out a career goal that is not aligned with your interests and personal mission, stop. The gut feeling you have is a signal that you are applying to the wrong opportunity, and the lack of authenticity will put your application at a disadvantage.

> **Tip: Exploring career tracks is not a career goal.**
>
> Don't mention in an application or interview that you are using the opportunity to explore careers, even if that is the case. The only time this type of response would work is if the mission of the organization is to help people explore career tracks, which is very rare. In any competition, you will be up against candidates who have specific career goals that are aligned with the organization's mission. If you tell the selectors that you do not already have a serious intent to work in the industry and will be there only to test your own interests, your application will go to the reject pile.
>
> © Pitch Your Potential / Vicki Johnson, Ph.D.

Proposing Highly Specific Projects

People who win fellowships, grants, and awards that require a research or project proposal tend to propose projects that are niche, meaning they are very narrow and focused, with a relatively small scope that capitalizes on the opportunity's unique benefits and the applicant's expertise. There are two benefits to this approach. First, niche projects are more memorable and eye-catching to selectors. Second, when a project has a narrow focus, it's easier to be highly specific and provide clear details about the timeline, resources, and execution needed to be successful. When the elements of mission alignment, timeliness, and urgency are added to the proposal, these niche ideas stand head and shoulders above those of other candidates.

Sometimes we believe that pitching a big, aspirational project with a broad scope is what selectors will invest in. Selectors do want projects that are impactful and newsworthy, but they are also concerned about feasibility. If you propose something that is too broad and pie-in-the-sky, without a clear explanation of how it will be completed successfully, the project will get rejected no matter how great it sounds. This happens when projects propose a person or group's involvement that is not guaranteed, requires resources that are not yet acquired, or requires a skill you don't have, like experience conducting research, among other possible setbacks to your project. Selectors don't want to risk investing in a project that might fail or end up incomplete because this hurts their return on investment.

To be highly specific, your project proposal for a competitive research grant, fellowship, residency, or business accelerator program should meet these six criteria:

1. It has a narrow research question or goal that is measurable.
2. It capitalizes on the unique benefits of the opportunity and the organization.
3. It is timely and urgent.
4. It is feasible given your skills, resources, and time to complete.
5. It is mutually beneficial.
6. It meets the needs and priorities of the funding body (i.e., it is mission-aligned).

Applicants should start with a project idea and narrow down the scope of the idea until it meets the six criteria. The best place to start is to consider your broad interests and, with those interests as a guidepost, look for ideas that would serve the needs and priorities of the organization providing the opportunity.

Case Study: An Example of a Highly Specific Project Proposal When developing a project for her Fulbright Visiting Scholar Award application to the United States, Australian scholar Dr. Kate Golebiowska started with a broad idea she had to create entrepreneurship resources for immigrant women in Darwin and narrowed it down to a highly specific project that could be executed only at her proposed U.S. host institution, Emory University in Atlanta, Georgia. Emory offered the unique benefit of having a program in place that could serve as a potential model for Darwin.

In her application, she wrote:

> *This Fulbright exchange with The Goizueta School of Business at Emory University will enable me to explore its business accelerator program, Start:ME, for immigrant-born women entrepreneurs and other under-represented groups in Atlanta. I will learn how a partnership between a university and not-for-profit partners can serve immigrant women seeking mentorship in entrepreneurship and, in a first for the Northern Territory, propose a framework to develop a similar program in Darwin.*

> *The R. Goizueta Business & Society Institute at the Emory Goizueta Business School delivers the [Start:ME] program free of charge . . . to new and aspiring micro-size business owners in three locations in Atlanta: Clarkston, East Lake, and Southside. The communities in which they are located have historically been home to immigrant and minority communities . . . . A decade worth of operation will be the ideal time to gain a deep insight into its enlargement, outcomes, and how the lessons learnt from the online delivery during the height of the COVID-19 pandemic are informing the post-pandemic program editions. These will be of utmost value because a combination of face-to-face and online delivery of training programs is gaining a foothold in Australia. Through this Fulbright project, I can directly experience the advantages as well as the challenges to creating a program like this at my home institution, CDU. My proposed stay in Atlanta from January to*

April 2023 would align with the 2023 cohort and allow me to engage with the program's community.

You'll notice in this project proposal that she addresses all the criteria for a niche project:

- **It has a narrow research question or goal that is measurable:** She proposed gathering lessons learned from the Start:ME program.
- **It capitalizes on the unique benefits of the opportunity:** The program is a university-nonprofit partnership that serves entrepreneurs from immigrant and minority communities similar to those in Darwin.
- **It is timely and urgent:** Her stay would align closely with the 2023 Start:ME cohort (urgent) and will provide lessons learned from the recent COVID-19 pandemic (timely).
- **It is feasible:** She provides a clear timeline of activities that appear feasible based on her expertise.
- **It is mutually beneficial:** The program could serve as a new model for implementation in Australia, benefiting both universities.
- **It meets the needs and priorities of the funding body (it is mission-aligned):** Later in her application, she discusses the long-term U.S.-Australia relationship the project would build, aligning with Fulbright's diplomatic mission.

The best way to create a niche project is to find out what projects the selectors want to see because they would benefit from their mission. It is easy to create a niche project proposal, but to be compelling for selection, you must be able to show how it is beneficial to all the stakeholders involved, including the funding organization, you, and groups and individuals who would be positively impacted.

Obtain Highly Specific References

It can be a huge advantage to your application or pitch to get recommendation letters or verbal references that are highly detailed. Often selectors will complain about brief or generic recommendation letters because they don't add any real value to an application. The value is in the detail of what this external party says about your accomplishments, motivations, personal drive, and integrity. Although you are not in control of what others say or do, you can increase your chances of getting a highly specific recommendation letter or reference by preparing your referees in advance with specific details of what to say about you.

When you need to provide recommendation letters or references, always prepare your selected referees to do this task well following these steps:

1. **Consider who would be willing to provide you with a positive reference.** This should be someone who has worked with you in some advisory capacity, such as a boss, professor, or head of an organization where you have volunteered. Do not discount those you have not connected with in many years; you can reconnect and prepare them for this favor!
2. **Identify a list of questions the selectors will likely ask the referee.** This might be a set list of questions in a recommendation letter prompt; you can ask the university or program to provide you with this prompt if it is not online. For job applications, look at the job description and consider what questions they might ask a referee. You can also ask an AI tool like ChatGPT to develop a list of possible reference questions based on the job description, as well as common questions asked of referees.
3. **Develop a list of bullet points of your projects, accomplishments, and responsibilities from the role that is related to each referee.** You'll provide this list of examples to your referee to prompt their memory and prepare them for

the questions that they might be asked. For a professor, this might be class projects and papers you wrote. For a boss, this might be projects you led, special assignments, and leadership roles.

4. **Ask your referee to meet in advance so you can go through the bullet points together.** This will ensure that the referee remembers and understands what you provided, and it may also prompt ideas for additional things to add.
5. **Provide your list in a digital folder with other necessary components,** including the recommendation letter instructions, your application, your résumé, and an empty business letter template addressed to the selection committee for them to fill in.
6. **Send reminders about the submission deadlines if applicable.** And of course, don't forget to thank them and keep them updated on your progress!

This seems like a lot, I know. But here's the thing: most applicants do not prepare their referees in this way; they only send them the instructions or alert them that someone might contact them and then hope for the best. Referees tend to be busy people who don't have a lot of time for special favors, which is why they might use a generic template or repurpose a letter they wrote for someone with a similar background. Those vague, generic letters written by tired, underappreciated referees are one of the primary reasons many candidates don't get selected.

It's your job to make the task of giving you a detailed reference as easy and enjoyable as possible. I know from experience that when you go above and beyond to prepare your referees, you will receive detailed letters and verbal references that will stand head and shoulders above those of your competitors. External references can go a very long way in sealing your selection because it is one of the only ways the selectors can validate the skills and accomplishments you state in your application.

Even more important, candidates have told me that when they prepared their referees in this way, the referees are so astounded and appreciative of the effort, they tend to say or write a reference letter that gushes with praise! This is another example of how the competitive application process itself has value regardless of the outcome. The process helps you stay connected with important people in your network, including guides and mentors, and builds your reputation of being highly prepared, thoughtful, and driven, leading to new opportunities you could not have imagined.

Key Takeaways

- Specificity is the art of curated detail. Specificity is noticed by selectors because it signals creativity, expertise, and vision.
- To stand out, remove platitudes, jargon, and other "fluff" from your pitch and replace it with simple language and high detail about your background, goals, and ideas.
- A highly specific MATCH ME Career Goal includes four components: (1) a specific type of role or position title, (2) at a specific type of organization (with a well-known example organization, if possible), (3) focused on a specific group you want to support or a specific problem you want to help solve, and (4) with a tangible outcome.
- Niche project proposals stand out and are easier to design. A niche project has a narrow research question or goal that is measurable; capitalizes on the unique benefits of the opportunity and the organization; is timely and urgent; is feasible given your skills, resources, and time to complete; is mutually beneficial; and meets the needs and priorities of the funding body (mission-aligned).
- Prepare your references by providing them with detailed information about you that they can include in recommendation letters and verbal references. By preparing them and

helping them save time, you'll build stronger relationships with these important members of your network.
- Wordsmithing using high detail is a skill that comes from practice. Practice specificity without the crutch of AI tools so that you can develop this skill for on-the-spot specificity in interviews, introductions, and negotiations.

Your Turn

Using the selective opportunity you are targeting, work on creating a MATCH ME Career Goal that aligns with the mission of the organization, including (1) a specific type of role or position title, (2) at a specific type of organization (with a well-known example organization, if possible), (3) focused on a specific group you want to support or a specific problem you want to help solve, and (4) with a tangible outcome.

7 | Make Your Pitch **Mutually Beneficial**

Show How You Win When They Win

When I first met Oumama Kabli, several years before her prestigious appointment as a U.S. Foreign Service Officer, she was a college graduate who was trying to figure out how to achieve her dream of becoming a diplomat. The U.S. Foreign Service is a sought-after public service career path with an intense selection process. Foreign Service Officers (FSOs) support U.S. embassies and consulates in high-level roles that involve negotiation, public relations, and complex problem-solving. Oumama was a smart, driven undergraduate student when she first applied for the U.S. Foreign Service, but when she undertook the Foreign Service Officer Test (FSOT), she failed. She told me that back then, she couldn't understand why she didn't pass. Yet, in that period, the FSOT had only a 22% pass rate. She would take the test two more times before she ultimately passed it several years later, learning a lot along the way.

Oumama's path through college is not a traditional one among people who enter the U.S. Foreign Service. Oumama immigrated to the United States at the age of 17, just before entering her senior year of high school in Northern Virginia. She was a top student. She applied and was accepted to George Mason University (GMU).

Unfortunately, within one semester, her parents could no longer pay her tuition. She immediately needed funding for college. So Oumama paused her studies to join the Virginia Army National Guard, an opportunity that would fund her education. After completing boot camp and advanced individual training, Oumama could not immediately go back to GMU because of an unpaid tuition bill. So she attended Northern Virginia Community College for two years and took advantage of the college's guaranteed transfer opportunity to GMU. Despite juggling school and two part-time jobs, she persevered and ultimately finished her undergraduate degree *summa cum laude*. This long and winding path to finishing college took an incredible amount of grit.

Oumama resolved to apply to the Foreign Service again, but she first focused on gaining more skills and knowledge through work experience. She won the opportunity to be a Fulbright English Teaching Assistant in Morocco for one year, and following this, she served as a contracts and grants officer at AMIDEAST, a U.S. nonprofit organization engaged in international education and development in the Middle East and North Africa. After working for a few years, Oumama was ready to pursue a master's in international affairs to prepare her for her next application to the U.S. Foreign Service. She found an extraordinary opportunity that was highly aligned with her goals and would help her meet the cost of graduate school: the

Thomas R. Pickering Fellowship. The Pickering Fellowship is a nationally competitive graduate award dedicated to "the principle that a broad range of perspectives strengthen diplomatic efforts and foster a comprehensive approach to global challenges."

The Pickering Fellowship is extraordinarily competitive. The award provides direct entrance to the U.S. Foreign Service and full funding for graduate study, a dual benefit that attracts thousands of applicants each year. The program selects just 45 Fellows annually based on demonstrated merit and financial need, resulting in a 3% acceptance rate. For this reason, Oumama had to give this application her all.

In working with me, Oumama learned the MATCH ME Formula® and how to use the formula to tell her story in writing and inspire the Pickering Fellowship selection committee. The personal statement prompt asked that she describe in one page her interest, motivation, and commitment to a career in international relations or public service; obstacles she had overcome; her cultural sensitivity; and her diverse interests and background. This is a lot to cover in just 500 words, and she had to be strategic in what to include and exclude and in her tone. Oumama told me, "Although I was not born and raised in America, I felt like I was living the American dream. And so in my statements, I aimed to convey that."

In describing how this fellowship would benefit her career goals, she wrote:

> *My long-term career goal as a Foreign Service Officer is to be actively engaged in implementing and supporting programs such as the Youth Exchange and Study Program, Global Undergraduate Exchange Program, and Fulbright. As someone who proudly wears my eclectic background on my sleeve, I believe that I can bring my unique diversity as a Muslim-American woman and firsthand experiences working in the capacity of a cultural ambassador to the ranks of the Foreign Service.*

I believe the best way I can make a tangible impact in this world is by continuing to promote global education through cultural exchange in the career track of a Public Diplomacy Officer. Looking forward, pursuing a master's degree in public policy or international education would give me the expertise to study the link between education and globalization and pursue independent research about its role in the Middle East and North Africa. The Pickering Fellowship would lessen the financial burden of a graduate education and provide me with mentorship opportunities, supported by individuals similarly interested and passionate about foreign service. I want to be a part of a community that works to promote peace and U.S. interests abroad in an environment where professionalism, mutual understanding, and diplomacy are highly valued. A career in the United States Foreign Service is the only way I believe I can give back to the country that has given me so much.

The Pickering Fellowship also asked candidates to provide a financial statement to allow the selection committee to understand their financial need, which would be compared to that of other candidates. Oumama had an important story of how she paid for her undergraduate studies independently of her parents, and this story helped demonstrate not only her financial need but her drive to attend college despite this financial hurdle.

For her financial statement of need, Oumama wrote:

The value of education has always been something instilled in me from a young age. From the time I graduated university, I knew that the only way I could advance my chances of working within the realm of international education or public policy would be to pursue a master's degree. I joined the Army National Guard on an 8-year contract to secure full funding for my undergraduate degree because I did not have any other sources of funding. . . . As a student, it took a huge burden off my back, allowing me to work full-time, intern, and attend required monthly trainings with the Guard, all while living on my own. Now that I have fulfilled my contract with the National Guard, I will not have the funding I need to pursue my graduate studies. Presently, the only two options I see are to: take out loans, which I believe would be extremely detrimental to my financial independence, and reenlist for another eight years in the Army. . . . Not only will this delay my ability to confer my degree in a timely manner; it will set me back in my three-year career plan, which includes completing a two-year full-time master's program, finishing my required internships, undergoing the security and financial clearance process, and entering the Foreign Service. . . . A Pickering Fellowship would allow me to fast-forward my career into the Foreign Service and provide me with opportunities outside of school to grow professionally and network with other foreign service experts.

Oumama's application fully applied all elements of the MATCH ME Formula®, securing her spot in the 2020 cohort of Pickering Fellows, which gave her a full tuition grant to pursue her master's at the top-ranked Johns Hopkins School of Advanced International Studies (SAIS). Oumama's selection for the fellowship reaped numerous benefits for them and her. It gave Oumama the financial ability to pursue a graduate degree and a guaranteed career pathway into the U.S. Foreign Service. Likewise, her selection fulfilled the Pickering Fellowship's mission to recruit highly qualified applicants who represent a broad range of American identities to the U.S. Foreign Service, needed to strengthen diplomatic efforts.

Oumama's application was very clear about why the fellowship funding for graduate study was integral to her ability to pursue a career in the U.S. Foreign Service. She explained her financial need clearly, particularly by emphasizing how she had joined the Army National Guard in order to pay for her undergraduate studies, a path few college students pursue. The Pickering Fellowship was the clear "hero" in her application story, expressing how it would help her achieve her academic and career goals. Her commitment to public service and resourcefulness in accessing undergraduate funding likely stood out among the hundreds of candidates who applied to the Pickering Fellowship with similar credentials.

Oumama's approach to her application exemplifies the second *M* in the MATCH ME Formula®, which stands for *Mutually beneficial*. **When a pitch is mutually beneficial, your application describes clear benefits to the organization and to you.**

For opportunities like the Pickering Fellowship, which considers need as well as merit, selectors will make their decisions based on which qualified candidates need the award most. For an opportunity like this, it is important to have a balance of information in your application that expresses why you are qualified to be selected based on your record of accomplishment and future potential, as well as why you need the award because of the hurdles you have faced in achieving your goals. Those hurdles may be higher for you than for other candidates, which supports your pitch for selection. For this reason, it's important to detail what your needs are and why those needs exist.

In this chapter, you will learn:

- Why mutual benefit matters
- How to express your financial, educational, and network needs

Why Mutual Benefit Matters

Organizations that offer graduate programs, fellowships, business accelerators, and awards want to place their investments where they can do the most good. In some cases, this means they will preference candidates who have not had access to similar opportunities, resources, and relationships in the past to achieve their goals. For this reason, it's important to tell selectors why you need their unique benefits, with supporting justification, and to show a track record of being responsible, resourceful, and hard working to demonstrate that you would be a good steward of their resources.

In previous chapters, I discussed ways to show how your selection is mutually beneficial by giving the selectors specific ideas of how you will help further their mission and goals if you are selected. By providing detailed ideas on how you will capitalize on their unique benefits, and relevant details from your background to demonstrate you have the skills and expertise to execute those ideas, you are able to make a compelling case as to why you should be selected. You also are able to demonstrate why the opportunity is beneficial to you—because it helps you achieve your future career goals and personal mission for social impact.

Here I discuss ways that you can address how the opportunity benefits you in regard to your personal needs. Your authentic need for the opportunity, based on your lack of access to opportunities, resources, and networks in the past, also helps make the case that the organization would be making an investment where it can do the most good if they select you.

Competitive programs and awards define need in different ways. Graduate programs will consider which candidates need the program most for their career and academic goals. Some fellowships, scholarships, and grants for academic study, professional development, and international exchange consider each candidate's personal financial need in addition to merit. There are also many competitive programs, including business accelerators and leadership programs, that support candidates who are underrepresented in their industry by race or gender because of historical discrimination. You'll also see selective programs offered for specific groups like military veterans, first-generation college students, immigrants, working parents and caregivers, people with disabilities, and other groups that lack opportunities and resources needed for their career advancement.

In some cases, the selectors' consideration of need is not stated in the program materials or application. When I have worked directly with fellowship organizations and graduate schools that are advertising their opportunities on ProFellow, some tell me that they do not want to recruit candidates who have already won other fellowships or similar awards because their goal is to give their opportunity to those who have not yet had one.

For programs that have a mission to address a gap in support for certain types of people, it's important you are clear that you are qualified for the opportunity based on your needs and provide specific examples of how the opportunity will benefit you. You can discuss in your pitch or application how you have faced limitations in achieving your professional and academic goals.

How to Express Your Personal Needs

First, you'll want to identify if the organization is considering your financial need or lack of access to opportunities through your mission research. When you find language that states they support underrepresented candidates in their mission statement or in the application materials like essay prompts, then you will know that increasing access to opportunities for underserved audiences is part of the organization's mission and goals. If they don't have any language to this effect, it does not necessarily mean they are not considering need in addition to merit. Fundamentally, many selection committees weigh which candidates have the most to gain from the opportunity when they narrow down their selection to a group of finalists.

For opportunities where you do meet the needs-based selection criteria and are aligned with the organization's mission, put time and effort into how you describe your need, being careful of your tone. When an opportunity is selective based on both merit and need, you are not going to be selected because you have the most need out of all the candidates. It is important, first and foremost, to show you are highly qualified based on the merit of your background and ideas for future impact. To help the selectors consider your needs, you should add details on your needs and how the opportunity will help you meet them in ways no other opportunity can.

How you express your personal needs is important because you want to say why you are deserving of the benefits, not entitled to them. To create this tone, you can describe why you appreciate the high value of the opportunity, how you will be a responsible steward of the benefits, and how the opportunity will help you make a positive impact on others in the future.

In the next sections, I provide some ideas on how to address your personal need for financial, educational, and network benefits.

Define Your Need for Financial Benefits

For most funding opportunities that consider candidates' financial needs, they want to meet the candidates' financial needs today, or support people who grew up low-income and faced financial hurdles early in their lives, or both. This is most common for academic opportunities like college and graduate school financial aid, merit-based graduate fellowships and scholarships, and funded professional development programs for people in low-paid fields like social services, education, and the creative arts.

If you grew up low-income and want to share this in your application without going into detail, you can include some simple signals in your pitch. For example, in higher education, it is well understood that someone who was a Pell Grant recipient had financial need for college. The Pell Grant is the largest federal grant program in the United States, providing college funding to undergraduate students from low-income households and those in the foster system. If you were a Pell Grant recipient, you might mention this briefly in your personal statement or résumé to signal some of the financial obstacles you faced while growing up.

You can also provide more explicit information about financial challenges you faced as a child, especially if those challenges hurt your ability to achieve your highest academic potential. I have met many applicants who shared how growing up low-income impacted their grades and SAT score, and consequently, where they went to college. Some students have less time for schoolwork and extracurriculars because they are working to support themselves or their families financially. For some, poverty, instability, and homelessness negatively impacted their physical and mental health and caused breaks or delays in finishing their studies. Many selectors empathize with the fact that young people do not begin on a level playing field and that a student's grades, low test scores, or short list of activities may not reflect their best academic abilities. It's important to tell these personal stories to help selectors justify your selection over other candidates who have a greater record of success but faced fewer obstacles.

In some cases, the selectors will want to know your financial need today, not just in the past. In the case of the Pickering Fellowship, candidates are asked to discuss in an essay why they need funding for graduate school. It's not enough to say you grew up low-income. Once you have graduated from college, you are considered a working-age adult. It's possible that today you have a high salary or savings or have an employer who offers grants for continuing education. You may have the ability to take on student loans. You may have a partner, family member, or friend who supports you financially. For all these reasons, even if you grew up low-income, your financial need might not be considered as significant as another candidate's. You must be able to show an authentic financial need now using highly specific examples.

Money is often considered a taboo subject, so it can be uncomfortable to provide a lot of details about your financial situation in an application read by strangers. Even your closest friends and family members may not know about your financial need, so you may struggle to put this statement together and get feedback on it. When this happens, just remind yourself of what you have to gain if you are selected and can access the financial support you need to achieve your goals. Be proud of the obstacles you have already overcome, and lean on examples of how you will be a good steward of the opportunities and unique benefits if you are selected.

Here are some items to include in your application to show financial need as an adult:

- **The amount of student loan debt you have from previous studies and your monthly payment.** To strengthen the description of need, explain what percentage the loan payment is of your monthly expenses. If your monthly payment is so high that it impacts your ability to comfortably pay your rent or mortgage, save for retirement, or pay for medical expenses, mention this.

- **Your salary and how it meets your living expenses.** Even if you have a higher-than-average salary, you may have very high living expenses because you live in an expensive area. If you have little to no disposable income after meeting your basic necessities, explain this in detail. Mention expenses like rent, childcare, health insurance, student and medical debt, food, transportation, and other expenses that impact your ability to save money or have disposable income for opportunities to advance your career.

- **How future student debt would impact your living expenses or ability to enter a career in public service.** Be sure to quantify the amount of debt you might face without the financial benefit offered by the organization and how that might impact your ability to raise a family, buy a home, or save for retirement. If your career goal is to enter a career track that does not pay high salaries, like teaching, social work, or academic research, discuss how future debt might affect your ability to pursue a career in service.

Keep in mind that without detail, selectors and other stakeholders can make assumptions about your financial choices; you do not want them to assume you were financially irresponsible if that is not the case. For example, if you are a U.S. veteran who has accrued a lot of student debt, selectors might wonder why you did not use the GI Bill, a federal program giving qualifying veterans money to cover all or some of the costs for school. The reason may be that you were not eligible or missed a window to use the award, so be sure to explain those reasons. Address all possible questions about your financial choices, debt, and expenses so selectors don't make the wrong assumptions. Whenever possible, show how you are making thoughtful financial choices to save money, like living with roommates, choosing public transportation over owning a car, or holding a second job to cover expenses. Mention if you proactively sought out other sources of funding that you were not able to access. If you have made money-saving sacrifices, such as choosing community college over a private university, be sure to include those. Showing a track record of responsible decision-making helps make the case for your selection.

Likewise, if you have made financial mistakes in the past, explain the mistake, what you have learned from the experience, and how you are making better decisions to improve your finances. If you are now mentoring others to help them avoid financial mistakes, mention this! Service to others can help strengthen your pitch and help overcome financial blemishes.

Note that for permanent jobs, it can work against you to discuss your financial need as a reason why you should be hired. Jobs are not created to provide people with salaries because people have expenses. You might feel tempted to mention that you really need the job because you are unemployed or behind on your bills. But your financial need is not a compelling reason to select you for a job; keep your pitch centered on the impact you can make in furthering the organization's mission and goals if you are selected. Once you receive an offer and have the opportunity to negotiate your starting salary, this is where an expression of your financial needs can help you negotiate for more pay, especially if you live in a high cost-of-living area, need to pay for transit or childcare to hold the job, or have student debt from a degree that helped qualify you for the position. Just keep in mind that the most effective way to negotiate for a higher salary is by expressing the value you bring to the organization, not your needs. So start your negotiation with the value you bring and why a higher salary would best reflect that value, and mention your personal financial needs as a second point.

Express Your Need for Educational Benefits

Competitive educational opportunities like graduate programs, professional fellowships, and business accelerators offering programming and mentorship sometimes prefer candidates who need the learning opportunities most to achieve their professional and academic goals. You might be highly qualified, but if you have already had many learning experiences in the field, selectors can assume the opportunity would be redundant. For this reason, it's important to explain why you can't get these educational benefits elsewhere and why they are critical to achieving your goals.

Here are some examples of showing the need for educational benefits:

- **The graduate degree is required for your future career goal.** For example, if you aim to be a physician, a medical degree is required. If you aim to become a lawyer, a law degree is required. Professions like university professor or scientist require a doctorate. In these cases, without the degree, your career goal cannot be achieved, so state this explicitly as your need, even if it seems obvious. In all other professions where a graduate degree is not required but very helpful, explain how the degree will prepare you and help you stand out when applying for your future dream job. You can explain how the lack of a degree can put you at a disadvantage or slow your progress toward achieving your goals.

- **The business accelerator is the only opportunity to learn key skills and access investors who can help your company grow quickly.** The reason they are called "accelerators" is because they provide programming and mentorship to help your business grow more quickly than you could on your own. State why you need the specific educational benefits that the accelerator offers and why these benefits are hard to access elsewhere, especially if you are from a group that is underrepresented in your industry.

- **The fellowship or grant is the only opportunity to get the funding or autonomy you need to complete a project, study abroad, or advance a skill.** Some competitive fellowships, international exchange programs, artist residencies, and other unique awards are designed to help you achieve a specific goal that is in alignment with the program's mission. Make sure to outline the specific educational benefits you would gain by accessing the award and how those benefits cannot be accessed elsewhere. For example, an international fellowship might be your only opportunity to undertake a study or research experience abroad.

This exercise of explaining your need for the educational benefits that the opportunity offers starts with your understanding of what the benefits are. Don't assume you know all the educational benefits. Do your mission research and take a look at how previous recipients have benefited from the program in unique ways so you can tie that into your pitch.

Show Your Need for Network Benefits

Virtually all dream jobs, awards, graduate programs, and other elite opportunities give you the benefit of expanding your network with leaders and peers in your industry. If you are a recent graduate who is new to the workforce or changing careers or have a business or project idea that would benefit from expertise outside your current network, you have a strong need to expand your network to achieve your personal mission and career goals. Consider what obstacles you face in building your network and how each opportunity is uniquely positioned to provide you with unique networking opportunities.

Here are some examples of when you would have a need for network benefits:

- **You are a graduating student and need help getting your foot in the door to your first job.** Competitive internships, professional and summer fellowships, and other programs designed for college students and recent graduates help young adults land their first permanent job. Being introduced to or interning with potential employers can be an important network benefit that you don't have access to now, so mention how you lack these opportunities without the program.

- **You need a broader network to execute a project, research, or a new business.** Think about the people you would meet if you are selected for the opportunity, and explain how you would not be able to build this network without the access, introductions, and caché of the opportunity. Networks can give you access to people who may be critical to your success.

- **You have lacked access to networks that provide intergenerational knowledge.** If you are the first in your family to go to college, work in an industry, start a business, or travel abroad, your parents may not have been able to provide you with the knowledge and tools on how to navigate these spaces. This is a network gap that might be filled by a special opportunity like a fellowship, leadership development program, or graduate program.

Case Study: How to Explain Network Benefits in a Pitch An excellent example of explaining network benefits comes from Jamaal Glenn, who successfully applied for the Marshall Memorial Fellowship, an elite program for an annual cohort of Americans. The selected Fellows participate in a 24-day fully funded tour in Europe, where they engage in high-level roundtables, seminars, alumni gatherings, and interactive sessions. The mission of the fellowship is to help emerging leaders from business, government, and civil society create new transatlantic networks and opportunities for collaboration. In the application, he was asked to explain in an essay (among other questions):

"How can the fellowship help you achieve your goals and/or overcome current challenges? How do you see opportunities for collaboration with the German Marshall Fund?"

He wrote:

My commitment to service was instilled in me early by my parents. My father was a city-government lawyer who died of Non-Hodgkin's lymphoma when I was ten years old. My mother is a retired grade school teacher. Yet, my deep commitment to improving the community around me didn't manifest itself until many years later. . . . My 18th birthday was the day after the controversial 2000 U.S. Presidential election. . . . I decided then that I wanted to one day run for office. But before running for office, I want to use technology, innovation, and financial capital to improve communities around the world and build bridges between them.

The logical next step in my career as a venture investor is to start my own investment firm. In the next few years, I will raise a $50 million venture capital fund. The fund will make early stage investments in entrepreneurs who are building solutions to solve problems that are impacting at least one billion people, with a particular interest in global *workforce development and the future of work, financial technology and services, education, mobility and logistics tools, and urbanization technology.... The Marshall Memorial Fellowship [MMF] is central to both my long and short-term goals. MMF alums, whom I've met through my previous transatlantic fellowships or through my involvement with organizations like the Council on Foreign Relations, rave about MMF as life-changing, while also praising the potency of its alumni community. I hope to leverage GMF and the MMF to make good on my promise to invest globally, sharpen my firm's expertise on markets in Europe and elsewhere, and to deploy capital in ways that align with smart policymaking. Eventually, when the time for public service comes, GMF can provide the platform from which my boldest, most forward-thinking policy ideas can grow.*

Without saying it directly, Jamaal explained some of the challenges he faced as a child, signaling that he did not have access to influential networks when he was growing up. But his parents, who both worked in service to others, inspired his goal to run for political office in the future. He discusses an immediate goal to raise a venture capital fund and how he would fully leverage the network benefits of the fellowship during and after the experience. This is a great example of explaining the need for unique network benefits to achieve a highly specific goal.

Even if you are someone who has not faced financial or educational hurdles, virtually everyone faces hurdles to building the right network to achieve their goals. If nothing else, explain that access to networks is a benefit you lack today and how this benefit will help you achieve your goals more quickly and effectively.

Paying the Benefits Forward

Need is nuanced. There are people who grow up with many privileges offered by their family's wealth, professional and business networks, university connections, and access to opportunities exclusive to certain groups. If you find yourself trying to make a case that you have a need and your explanation feels inauthentic, it probably is. No matter what your personal situation is, consider the privileges that were provided to you without qualification or effort, and choose to bypass opportunities that were not designed for someone with your advantages.

But remember that no one chooses the family or circumstances they were born into, so we all have a mix of advantages and disadvantages that are outside of our control. Someone's greatest privilege, like family wealth, might be a weak advantage to achieving success compared to someone who grew up poor but has the privilege of a supportive family offering unconditional love and attention. You will never know just by looking at someone's grades, universities, job titles, income, gender, or race what advantages or disadvantages they have faced.

When you win a dream job, award, or elite opportunity, I hope you will feel inspired to pay the benefits forward by sharing your skills and experiences with the application process with those who can benefit from your insider knowledge. When we share our skills, offer introductions in our networks to new applicants, engage in alumni programming, and serve as mentors to the next generation, we create a long-lasting legacy of impact and make the benefits we received accessible to others.

For me, the public schools I attended while growing up had many problems and lacked the resources to prepare me well for college. But, without any effort on my part, I had the advantage of being raised by two resourceful and loving parents who provided me enough knowledge and skills to help me attend college and seek out career opportunities and mentors as I went into the workforce. I know many young people don't have the advantage of engaged parents. This book is my way of paying forward the privileges and opportunities I had in the hope of helping you achieve your biggest goals.

> **Tip: There will be a time when you transition from applying to opportunities to creating your own.**
>
> When you have reached a stage in your career where you have already achieved multiple fellowships, awards, or graduate degrees, you may hit a plateau and start facing more rejections for similar programs and awards, because the selectors are not convinced that you need the opportunity more than other candidates. This is the stage when you need to be more strategic about which opportunities you pursue and start identifying ways to create your own opportunities for career growth and project funding. After winning four fellowships myself, I stopped applying to fellowships and focused on creating my own opportunities by becoming an entrepreneur and founding ProFellow. Through entrepreneurship, I raised my own revenue, created a leadership role for myself, and developed an organization focused on achieving my personal mission to connect service-oriented emerging leaders with opportunities for their career growth.
>
> © Pitch Your Potential / Vicki Johnson, Ph.D.

Key Takeaways

- Many selectors will preference qualified applicants who have the most to gain from their opportunity. In your mission research, look for language in their mission statement or application materials that indicates if need is part of their selection criteria.
- A pitch that is mutually beneficial describes clear benefits to the organization and to you. Your authentic need for the benefits helps make the case that the organization is making an investment where it can do the most good.

- For opportunities that consider financial need, don't allow the selectors to make assumptions about your financial situation and choices. Be very clear about the challenges to meeting your monthly expenses now or in the future, and demonstrate that you will be a good steward of financial benefits if you are selected.
- Some opportunities consider who needs their educational and network benefits most. Discuss how these benefits cannot be accessed elsewhere and how they will help you achieve your goals more quickly.
- People who have several similar awards or degrees may have a hard time making a compelling case based on need. If you are in this position, consider whether it is time to pursue different types of opportunities or find ways to create your own.
- When you win a dream job, award, or elite opportunity, pay the benefits forward through sharing your knowledge with the next generation of applicants.

Your Turn

For the opportunity you are targeting, look for language that indicates if the organization is considering need in addition to merit in their selection criteria. Using the examples in this chapter, describe in detail why you need the financial, educational, or network benefits the opportunity provides.

8 | Master **Elegance**

Balance Your Tone with Self-Confidence and Humility

I first began working with Erin Gallagher when she was in her early 30s and sought to make the leap to graduate school after an early career with a winding path. She grew up in Charlotte, North Carolina, and graduated from the University of North Carolina–Wilmington *summa cum laude* but was burnt out. Instead of taking a traditional entry-level job, she worked as a nanny for a summer and then, through the advice of a mentor, undertook a one-year English teaching job in France.

Still working through uncertainty about her career, Erin had an opportunity to visit with a mentor, a professor she studied under, and her professor's father, a retired farmer, while in France. The older farmer spoke about the farm and the challenging impacts of increasing temperatures and climate change. Erin said she had a "Eureka moment" that would spark a decade-long interest in global food systems, a topic that combined her interests in international affairs, environmental policy, and health. Afterward, she began to read books, attend events, talk with experts, and volunteer her time to learn more about the subject. She was beginning to develop a clear and specific personal mission.

At that time in 2017, there were few entry-level jobs she could pursue to build on this interest in food systems. She was able, however, to spend one year at the Capital Area Food Network of North Carolina as an AmeriCorps VISTA member. Following this position, she made a practical pivot and worked in law firms supporting business development and marketing, which gave her a steady paycheck and transferable skills. These jobs did not have the mission focus she desired, so she sought out every opportunity to support the small portion of the firm's initiatives related to environmental, social, and governance issues.

For several years, Erin considered pursuing a graduate degree (and she dreamed of going back overseas), but she kept putting the idea off, particularly once the pandemic hit. When she decided it was finally time to go to graduate school in 2024 to study food systems, nine years after her undergraduate degree, she was worried about being an oddball candidate because of her age and lack of professional experience in the subject. She was also concerned about the cost of graduate school after facing financial insecurity at different points in her life. So she made it a goal to apply to competitive graduate programs abroad, and to fund her studies, she would apply to the small number of competitive international graduate funding awards available to Americans.

Erin admitted to me that she felt very overwhelmed as she tried to navigate these goals alone. As she worked with me, Erin learned how to interpret and apply the MATCH ME Formula® as she prepared her applications. To be more competitive, she did in-depth mission research on each school to narrow her sights on a few graduate programs abroad that were highly aligned with her goals, including the Master in Agroecology and Food Sovereignty at the University of

Gastronomic Sciences in northern Italy and the Master of Arts in Food Studies at the American University of Rome.

She also applied for a Rotary Global Grant, a highly competitive graduate funding award for study abroad that is funded by the international Rotary Foundation and administered by local Rotary clubs throughout the United States. The Rotary Global Grant is one of the few nationally competitive grants that help Americans fund graduate study abroad. The award receives more than 1,000 applications each year, but less than 20% of applicants are selected to receive the scholarship.

Erin worked hard to prepare a strategic application story for her Rotary Global Grant application and spent many hours investigating the mission and history of Rotary, an international organization and network dedicated to community and public service. Global food security is one of the challenges the Rotarian mission seeks to address, making the grant aligned with her goals. Yet she worried that her background would not be competitive enough to beat out the hundreds of other applicants applying for this unique award.

Before learning the MATCH ME Formula®, Erin mentioned that she would have tried to emphasize her undergraduate GPA and all her professional accomplishments to "prove" she was qualified and worthy of the award. In her previous mindset, she thought of the selectors as judges who would decide if she was deserving of selection. She felt she could not be modest about her accomplishments when making her pitch.

But after learning the MATCH ME Formula®, both her mindset and approach to her applications changed. She decided to focus fewer words in her personal statement on her background and more words on her desire to apply her skills and talents to food security in the future, to positively impact others, in order to show how her personal mission aligned with the Rotary mission. She also included words on how she would be an engaged grantee and Rotary award alumna long after her graduate studies to demonstrate her commitment to remaining an active member of Rotary's global network.

This future-facing emphasis in her application paid off, and she was selected as a finalist by her local Rotary Club in Chapel Hill, North Carolina. Yet the process was not over: she still had to undertake three intense, multi-hour interviews to help the selection committee choose a winner.

In the final interview, the committee stumped her momentarily with a question she hadn't prepared for: "Give us one word to describe yourself." After a moment of reflection, digging deep into the treasure chest of knowledge she had developed about herself and her alignment with the mission of Rotary, she responded: "I should probably say ambitious or driven or high-achiever, but I'm going to say *optimist*." She went on to describe her reasons: "When it comes to food systems and the environment, everything looks pretty bad right now, but I have optimism that I can help make a difference. This is what drives me to devote my career to this work."

With that, Erin effectively pitched her potential with one elegant word: *optimist*.

When she got the congratulatory call, the representative of the Rotary Global Grant selection committee told her that her response to this final question was what sealed their decision to select her among the short list of exceptional finalists.

Why did the word *optimist* matter to the selection committee? Because it expressed her self-confidence that she could contribute significantly to Rotary's mission and positively impact others. She also displayed humility in choosing to describe herself as hopeful rather than ambitious.

Erin's commitment to her personal mission and how she expressed it was the edge to her pitch that compelled the selection committee to choose her over other very qualified and committed applicants. She has now achieved an extraordinary career dream. In 2025, Erin is completing her Master of Arts in Food Studies with full funding at the American

University in Rome, while building a new global network and charting a path toward a career in global food systems and sustainability.

Erin's balanced approach to her application exemplifies the letter *E* in the MATCH ME Formula®, which stands for *Elegant*. In this case, **elegance is defined as the careful balance of self-confidence and humility in an application.**

When you achieve elegance in how you express yourself, especially when speaking about yourself and your goals, you will not fear being judged for sharing your accomplishments, and you will not view the outcome of the competition as a reflection of your worth.

In this chapter, you will learn:

- What elegance is and why it matters
- How a winner's mindset creates elegance
- Three strategies to become naturally elegant in your applications

What Elegance Is and Why It Matters

Elegance is the careful balance of self-confidence and humility, giving a tone that communicates *dignified grace* in your speaking, writing, or appearance. Elegance is a sign of high emotional intelligence (EQ) and reflects personality traits like self-awareness, poise, empathy, and compassion. Candidates who display elegance in their applications send the underlying message that they treat others (and themselves) with respect and dignity, apply inner strength to challenging situations, and are able to build and maintain trust. It signals they will be a pleasure to work with. On the other hand, candidates who lack elegance in the tone of their application and come off as either arrogant or overly modest can cause selectors to believe they have a low EQ and may be difficult to work with.

In his bestselling book, *Emotional Intelligence: Why It May Matter More Than IQ*, Daniel Goleman (2005) lays out why high emotional intelligence is important in leadership. High EQ is the ability to control one's own emotions and perceive and respond responsibly to others' emotions, which facilitates stronger interpersonal communications and relationships and better decision-making. Those with low emotional intelligence tend to struggle to build strong personal and professional relationships, don't respond well to social cues, and have difficulty accepting constructive criticism.

For this reason, selectors will choose people with high EQ, especially for opportunities that require leadership or self-sufficiency; trust with financial resources; or engagement with their staff, clients, and stakeholders. Even with high grades, test scores, and other accomplishments, people with poor emotional intelligence have a hard time getting selected over candidates who exhibit a balance of self-confidence and humility.

Selectors are assessing your emotional intelligence both consciously and unconsciously when they read your written application, cover letter, pitch, or proposal. They will also assess your EQ in mutual or self-introductions and through the interview process. For this reason, you want to be strategic in the tone of your applications and introductions and exhibit elegance.

The skill of displaying elegance in your choice of words in your written application or verbal pitch comes from having the right mindset about the competition. You will naturally become more elegant in how you pitch yourself for an opportunity when you:

- View your selectors as future collaborators, not judges who are deciding your worth
- Are grateful to be considered for access to unique benefits and resources
- Have a personal mission that positively impacts others

These ingredients are the basis of the *winner's mindset* that I describe in the introduction of this book. The winner's mindset is not the belief that you are better than other contenders, which leans toward superiority and arrogance. Rather, it is the belief that you deserve and can achieve the opportunity because you have applied your highest effort to the application. When you have self-confidence about what you can contribute, as well as the humility that there are many other talented people in the competition, you'll feel that the competition is about a lot more than just acceptance and rejection; it's an opportunity to learn, build your network and skills, and go after your biggest dreams. For someone with a winner's mindset, the only failure is not trying.

Selectors are looking for people with a winner's mindset because these people have high emotional intelligence and the confidence to pursue high goals. Your winner's mindset is expressed through the elegance you display in your choice of words and actions throughout the selection process.

How a Winner's Mindset Creates Elegance

A lot of our cultural tropes about winning are based on concepts about individualism, dominance, and finality. You might associate the word *win* with common phrases like *winner takes all*, *play to win*, and *go big or go home*. The tone of these phrases gives the message that superiority matters and that winning an opportunity is an individualistic pursuit that must have losers. But to be successful at winning dream jobs, awards, top graduate school spots, and other elite opportunities, this type of attitude toward the competition can hold you back because the conditions for selection are out of your control.

In a marathon, the winner is a person who is measurably the fastest. As a competitor, you have ultimate control over your speed and the outcome of the race. In this case, you might fear your competitors, but you don't fear a selector because the winner is chosen by something that is clear, fair, and objective: a clock.

In the competitions of your career, you have no real control over the outcome because you are judged by a person or committee on subjective factors like leadership potential, intelligence, skills, and the perceived value of your ideas. The selectors have control over who wins, and they typically make their decisions behind closed doors, shrouded in secrecy. This subjectiveness, secrecy, and our lack of control over the selection process are what cause us to fear and resent selectors. This fear and resentment of selectors, combined with an individualistic *winner takes all* attitude, creates negative energy toward others that impacts the choice of words we use in our applications and interviews.

Some candidates fear selectors and the competitive application process because they struggle to show self-confidence in an application. They are deeply impacted by comparison culture and have an outsized fear that other contenders have better résumés and are more likely to win. Candidates with low confidence have a hard time expressing why they should be selected, because they really don't know. This lack of confidence causes them to sabotage their best efforts and show up poorly in interviews, even with preparation.

Other candidates are overconfident. They believe their credentials, prestigious schools, job titles, business success, or connections make them a shoo-in for the opportunity. This belief is dangerous because overconfident candidates tend not to put their absolute best effort into the application. They also show up poorly in interviews because they do little to prepare; they feel confident they can "wing it" and succeed.

Both types of candidates—the unconfident and the overconfident—do poorly in high-stakes competitions for elite opportunities because they are unprepared and view the competition and their contenders in a negative way. But even if you start off unconfident or overconfident, it's possible to reach the balance of self-confidence and humility that signals high emotional intelligence through intense preparation for the competition.

Self-confidence is borne from the feeling that you deserve the opportunity because of the high effort you put into your application and the compelling vision you created of your future potential in the process. When you are self-confident, you are excited to share this vision, which is grounded in your skills, talents, and unique lived experience.

Humility is borne from respecting your competitors and recognizing that some of them may be deserving of the opportunity too. Rather than worrying about what your competitors will bring, you focus on putting your best foot forward using the skills, resources, and tools you have available to you. When you have humility and lose to a competitor, you congratulate them—and mean it.

Self-confidence and humility are positive human emotions that create *elegance* in how you speak about yourself and others in a way that helps you build relationships and stand out as a top candidate.

You can make use of three strategies to become naturally elegant in your answer to the question "Why you?" in your application or pitch: (1) nix calling yourself the "best" candidate, (2) recognize that accomplishments are evidence, not self-praise, and (3) have empathy for your selectors.

Nix Calling Yourself the "Best" Candidate

If you find yourself making statements in your job applications, personal statements, or interviews that you are the "best" or "perfect" candidate for an opportunity, you are not alone. The question is, do you really believe that? Because you don't actually know much, if anything, about the candidates you are up against! Second, you don't know the selectors well enough to perfectly understand what they are looking for in a candidate (and in fact, they may not know themselves).

From early in our careers, there's an unspoken expectation that we make a confident expression that we are the "best" candidate for a selective opportunity. One of the most common interview questions of all time is: "Tell us why you are the best candidate for the job." We are then prompted to say, "I'm the best candidate because . . ." and fill in the response with a long list of skills and experiences we would bring to the role.

There is nothing technically wrong with this response, especially when it is so explicitly prompted. But you should never assume that this question means the selectors are looking for a bold, assertive response. In some cases, you may misunderstand what they are looking for and even make the mistake of walking into a trap of looking overconfident.

I recommend taking a different approach that incorporates elegance: acknowledging that there are other highly qualified candidates for the opportunity and then stating why you are different (not the best). This is an elegant way to show respect for others and respect for the selectors' decision.

I once worked with a candidate who first drafted his cover letter for a leadership position filled with overconfident language. He wrote:

> *I'm the best candidate for this position because I have been preparing for it my whole life. I earned a top business degree from the Loyola University Quinlan School of Business, have five years of experience leading teams at a Fortune 500 company, and have earned several prestigious awards for innovation from my superiors. I know I have what it takes to take this role to the next level.*

I encouraged him to soften this language to provide more specific details that would signal his accomplishments as being "top" and "prestigious" without saying so directly to display elegance. I also recommended he nix the statement about being the "best" candidate.

Here's how he updated the statement:

> *I have prepared in a number of ways for this unique opportunity to lead a team of 20 and advance the company's newest product line. At Loyola, I learned through the Business Honors Program how to apply integrated analytical decision making, which I used in my role as Senior Director, managing a growing remote team and helping us achieve 20% year-over-year revenue growth. This past year, I was recognized with my second innovation award for my idea that evolved into the company's now leading product line. I'm excited to apply my experience and skills to a new opportunity at your company.*

This statement generally says the same thing but with more detail and fewer adjectives that might be perceived as overconfident.

Recognize That Accomplishments Are Evidence, Not Self-Praise

Candidates who are uncomfortable speaking about themselves and sharing their accomplishments may have grown up in an environment where it is culturally unacceptable to brag. In some cultures, people are even criticized, bullied, or resented for being "too" successful, a phenomenon some people call "tall poppy syndrome." I experienced this firsthand when I studied abroad in New Zealand, which has a well-known "tall poppy" culture.

If you grew up in a family or community where you were criticized for achieving success or speaking about your accomplishments, you may have never developed the skills and practice to respond confidently when a selector asks, "Why you?" This discomfort pitching yourself can also stem from impostor syndrome, the feeling that your accomplishments are undeserved, as well as from discouragement from mentors and comparing yourself to your peers.

If you feel uncomfortable writing a cover letter or essay about yourself or speaking confidently about your achievements in an interview, it's because you have been conditioned to believe that speaking about your accomplishments is a sign of arrogance. It's time to break this agreement. By allowing this belief to negatively impact your ability to compete, you subjugate yourself to people-pleasing behavior that actually pleases no one.

Except for lifetime achievement awards and honorary degrees, the selective jobs, university spots, fellowships, and business accelerators you apply to are not awards for what you have done in the past but investments in what you will do in the future. Selectors need hard evidence that you have the skills, educational training, ideas, and experiences they are looking for in order to make a decision to invest in you. When you downplay your accomplishments to be modest, you hurt your chances of collaborating with them in the future. You are not pitching your potential but pleasing an outside group of people who do not hold the resources you need to achieve your goals.

Therefore, remind yourself regularly of this key point, which should appeal to those of you who care deeply about the feelings and needs of others: **when you talk about your accomplishments in an application for a selective opportunity, it is not self-praise; you are providing hard evidence that you have the experience, skills, and motivation needed to contribute to their mission and make the best use of their investment.**

If you focus on serving the needs of your selectors, treating them like future collaborators rather than judges, you can confidently provide them with clear and compelling reasons why you are a good investment with their limited resources. Also remember why you are applying for the opportunity: to advance your personal mission to solve a problem experienced by others. By providing your accomplishments as evidence of your hard work and commitment, you are working to gather the resources and skills you need to make a greater social impact on others in the future.

If you still struggle to express your accomplishments because you grapple with impostor syndrome and don't believe you are as skilled and talented as you appear on paper, it's time for you to do some deep reflection on what is true. Because of comparison culture and the pressure of gatekeepers who advise us to lower our goals, we are afraid to use the wrong words to describe ourselves because, deep down, we worry that our positive opinions of ourselves won't be believed. This is a form of perfectionism that will hold you back from putting in your highest effort.

To overcome self-limiting beliefs, challenge yourself to ask your boss, your professors, your peers, and your family and friends what they believe are your strengths and talents. When they tell you, ask them why, and listen closely. These ideas are coming from others who are viewing you in the best way possible, and you can increase these positive messages by improving your effort in everything you do. Remember the obstacles you have overcome and remind yourself of the many moments of self-doubt that you pushed through to achieve a degree, land your first job, make new friends, or complete a personal goal. Self-confidence is a muscle that takes practice. Feed your brain with positive messages about your talents, knowledge, and skills to train your brain to feel pride in what you have achieved.

Have Empathy for Your Selectors

Finally, remember that selectors are people too. Often, we look at people on selection committees as feared judges who are deciding our worth through their acceptance or rejection. You'll become more motivated to prepare an exceptional application and will receive more positive results when you start to view your selectors as friends and future collaborators, rather than judges.

Selectors are spending their time and effort distributing limited opportunities and resources to get the best possible results from their investments, which support their organization's mission. Like you, selectors also have a goal and responsibility to be successful in their choices. Although they are the ones holding the cherished opportunity, which seems like a great privilege that we lack, they are not benefiting from the opportunity in the way you are. Their role is different. They are working under the expectations of others and being judged for their success or failure in choosing the best candidates.

If you receive a rejection, it may not be because of what you provided, but because of what you *didn't* provide in writing or in your interview. It's possible that your application lacked memorable information, compelling ideas, or enough detail about your background and future goals necessary to make it possible for them to select you!

Yet we often take a rejection to mean we just aren't good enough. This causes us to feel fearful and resentful, rather than grateful, toward selectors, especially after we have experienced several rejections. A series of rejections can harden these negative feelings, which can then lead to more negative outcomes because we are now in a fog of disappointment and uncertainty that influences our actions.

There is great power in viewing your selectors with empathy and appreciation and incorporating gratitude to acknowledge their time and consideration into your application. Just like the power of memorable stories, there's something deeply moving about an authentic "thank you" that is ingrained in our human DNA. If you recognize the power of gratitude, you can leverage this positive feeling to make your application stand out.

 Tip: Incorporate a brief note of gratitude in every communication to selectors.

A simple way to express your gratitude to selectors is to incorporate the sentence "Thank you for your consideration" somewhere in your application. This might come as a stand-alone line at the end of a personal statement or the final line in your job cover letter. Also express gratitude in introductions and interviews. Finally, don't forget to send a thank-you email to the members of the selection committee after every interview.

© Pitch Your Potential / Vicki Johnson, Ph.D.

For every competition you enter, imagine that your goals and the selectors' goals are the same. Both sides want to collaborate so that together you can make the greatest social impact possible, combining your talents with their resources. Imagine that the selection committee is on your side—they want you to win and enthusiastically invite you to apply! But your responsibility is to give them what they need to make this collaboration feasible. So help them by helping yourself: be the most prepared applicant in the competition who delivers an aligned, memorable, highly specific, and impact-driven pitch that makes it easy for selectors to say "Yes!" Make them feel confident in their decision to choose you and resolve to make them look good once you are selected.

Key Takeaways

- Elegance is the careful balance of self-confidence and humility in your application. This tone signals to selectors that you have high emotional intelligence (EQ) and personality traits like self-awareness, poise, empathy, and compassion.
- Think of selectors as future collaborators and friends rather than judges. Their decisions do not determine your worth or merit.
- Instead of calling yourself the "best" or "perfect" candidate, demonstrate why you are different and provide the best examples of your skills, talents, and commitment.
- Remind yourself that detailing your accomplishments is not self-praise. This detail provides selectors the evidence they need to make a difficult decision on how to invest their limited time and resources.
- Incorporate the sentence "Thank you for your consideration" somewhere in your job, fellowship, or graduate school application.
- Help selectors by being the most prepared applicant in the competition and providing them a detailed and inspirational pitch.

Your Turn

Take these steps to make your application more elegant:

1. Review your application for language that might signal overconfidence, such as describing your own accomplishments as "prestigious."
2. Replace vague language summarizing your background, which can signal a lack of confidence, and replace it with text that details your relevant skills and experiences that provide hard evidence you are prepared for the role.
3. Find a place in your application to add the line "Thank you for your consideration" to express authentic gratitude to the selectors for their time and the opportunity they are offering you as an applicant.

9 | Apply the MATCH ME Formula®

Put the Full Formula to Work in Your Pitch

I hope the MATCH ME Formula® elements and the stories of success have ignited your excitement to apply these strategies in your next competition. This chapter is designed to help you bring all of these elements together in your next personal pitch.

The MATCH ME Formula® is a combination of mindset and tactical strategies that will help you stand out in the competitions of your career. As you apply to dream jobs, awards, and elite opportunities, it will help you achieve greater self-confidence and become a master at persuasive communication. It will also help you build your professional network and reputation as a candidate who goes above and beyond in each competition. If you commit to using the MATCH ME Formula®, you'll find yourself being tapped for extraordinary, word-of-mouth opportunities in the future that you cannot imagine now.

Future success starts with your winner's mindset. It is critical that you are aware of the mental and external hurdles that will hold you back from choosing the right opportunities and putting in your highest effort. To recap, these are the actions to develop your winner's mindset:

- **Identify your personal mission, which is your pursuit of a goal that helps solve a problem experienced by others.** If you have no clear mission at this moment because you have many interests, focus on opportunities with a mission that excites you, where you can apply your talents and skills to make a positive impact on others. When you have a personal mission and pursue opportunities that align with your mission, you'll have a career that is adventurous and personally fulfilling, helping you achieve your own definition of "success."

- **Commit to being the most prepared applicant in the competition.** Ignore discouragement from gatekeepers. Don't concern yourself with your competitors' résumés and the low success rates for elite opportunities. Only concern yourself with being the most prepared applicant you can be, using the resources, people, knowledge, and experiences you have available to you. When you are a highly prepared applicant, you exponentially increase your chance of selection over other highly qualified candidates. Even if you don't achieve the opportunity, you will make a positive impression on your references and on the selectors in ways that will build your reputation and network.

- **Cultivate your relationship with guides who encourage you to strive for big goals.** Guides are people who have useful experience and knowledge about the opportunities that interest you and who encourage you to pursue big, aspirational goals. They will support and celebrate your high effort. They will also tell you to improve the effort and try again if you face a rejection. Unlike gatekeepers, guides build your self-confidence, courage, skills, and grit.

- **Exclusively apply to opportunities for which you have mission alignment and that you authentically desire.** Be sure to do research on the mission and goals of the organization offering the opportunity, and reflect on whether this mission is aligned with your personal mission and would help you achieve your deepest desires and goals for your life. Authentic desire for an opportunity is a key advantage.

With a winner's mindset, you can successfully apply the seven elements of the MATCH ME Formula®. As you begin to use them to prepare applications, cover letters, proposals, and business pitches, you'll build the confidence that you are a highly prepared applicant and will better understand how the seven elements are mutually reinforcing.

To recap, MATCH ME stands for:

M = Memorable
A = Aligns with the organization's mission
T = Timely
C = Capitalizes on the organization's unique benefits
H = Highly specific
M = Mutually beneficial
E = Elegant

Not only does MATCH ME encapsulate the seven individual elements of a winning application, but the words *Match Me* represent the power of matching your personal mission and goals with the mission and goals of the selectors who provide dream jobs, awards, and elite opportunities.

In this chapter, you will learn:

- How to create your winning application story
- Three frameworks to help you apply the MATCH ME Formula® to a cover letter, personal statement, and interview prep
- Guiding questions to apply the MATCH ME Formula®

How to Create Your Winning Application Story

For each competitive opportunity that you apply for, you'll want to create the outline for your winning application story that will serve as a guidepost as you create each component of your application and prepare for interviews and other engagements with selectors. Your *application story* is the succinct response to the question "Why you?" for competitive opportunities that have many other candidates. Having an application story for each opportunity helps ensure that you stay on message and avoid vague, confusing, or conflicting information as you prepare a multitude of components for your pitch, including a résumé, cover letter, essays, short answer responses, and project proposal. The application story also guides how you speak about yourself and your goals in interviews and informal conversations with selectors.

The application story is particularly important when you are applying at once to multiple opportunities that have different missions and unique benefits. The application story makes each opportunity appear like it is "the one" for you when consumed by a selection committee because it is highly tailored to them and demonstrates high effort and authentic desire.

A winning application story has a beginning, a middle, and an end. The beginning and the end of the story address the two most common questions selectors will ask about you: "What are your goals?" and

"What is your background?" Often, you will discuss the beginning and end of the story first in your written applications and interviews. The middle "hook" is the most critical piece of the application story, often discussed last in your pitch for emphasis. The "hook" explains how the opportunity serves as the bridge from where you are now to where you want to be in the future.

To recap the application story arc:

- The **beginning** is your background up until this point, supported with memorable personal anecdotes that explain the motivations behind your career choices and your key characteristics that they look for in candidates, such as leadership, creativity, intellectual curiosity, and a commitment to service.
- The **end** of the story is in the future, after the opportunity. The end is the achievement of your highly specific and timely goal, which has a positive impact on others that fulfills both your ambition and personal mission and the organization's mission, making your selection mutually beneficial. This part of the story defines your future potential and is used to help you stand out and inspire selectors.
- The **middle**, the story "hook," is where you couch the organization as the "hero" needed to help you advance from where you are now to where you want to be in the future. You express how the organization offers two to three unique benefits that you will capitalize on to achieve your future goal that also advances their mission. Your key message is: *without their unique benefits, the goal may not be achieved.*

To provide an example of a compelling application story arc, imagine you are applying to a top graduate school for a master of public policy after working for three years on housing policy at a local government agency. Your goal is to work at a higher level in housing policy. Your winning application story might look something like this:

> **The Story Beginning (Your Background):** *Throughout my academic and professional career, I have been preparing for a leadership role in public service with a focus on housing policy, beginning with my childhood interest in service-related opportunities like Girl Scouts and student government, to the selection of my college major, political science, to my entry into a local government role where I have contributed to efforts to support the creation of affordable housing in my home town.*
>
> **The Story End (Your Goal):** *My future goal is to enter a senior analyst role at the federal level, working in the U.S. Department of Housing and Urban Development or a contributing policy think tank, where I can apply the skills, knowledge, and perspectives I have gained at the local level to help craft effective federal policies to increase affordable housing nationally. During graduate school, I aim to gain skills in economics and policy analysis to develop research that measures the effectiveness of local housing policies, such as changes to zoning, rent stabilization, and homeless shelter subsidies, using AI technology.*
>
> **The Middle "Hook" (Why Them):** *General University's Master in Public Policy, with a subfocus on housing policy, is the ideal program for my career goals because of its innovative coursework on the application of artificial intelligence for policy analysis that I have not found elsewhere. The university's research institute on private-public partnerships and its relationship with the local city council, where the university is contributing to housing policy in real time, are unique opportunities that I would aim to become involved with if I am selected for the program. I would choose the option to complete a research thesis in my second year in order to advance my research skills and develop my academic network with faculty who are researching housing policy throughout the country.*

As an applicant, you can use an application story like this as a guidepost for creating an exceptional personal statement and preparing for an interview with the university. If you were an applicant with this example application story, here are some of the ways you could incorporate the MATCH ME Formula®:

- Add a **memorable** opening story to your personal statement about being a Girl Scout that demonstrates a commitment to public service since childhood.
- Show **alignment** with the graduate school's training mission to prepare students for careers in housing policy.
- Emphasize your **timely** focus on today's greatest housing challenges, mentioning specific current events and the urgency of gaining these skills now to help address these challenges.
- Describe how you will **capitalize** on at least three unique benefits of the university that cannot be accessed elsewhere.
- Be **highly specific** by using detail when describing your background, career goals, and the graduate program's unique benefits.
- Explain how your selection is **mutually beneficial** to the university's mission to train future housing policy leaders and your personal mission to help solve housing challenges.
- Display **elegance** by avoiding overconfident language and adding a final, stand-alone line to your personal statement: "Thank you for your consideration."

Three Frameworks to Help You Apply the MATCH ME Formula®

What follows are three frameworks for applying the MATCH ME Formula® to cover letters, personal statements, and interview prep. These frameworks are intended to show you how to create documents using the seven MATCH ME Formula® elements. You may use the components of these frameworks in a different order, and in some cases, you may need to subtract or add components to your application based on the application questions. Whenever you are applying for an opportunity with a formal application process, be sure to carefully review the questions they might ask and consider how to lay out your answers so that they embody your full application story and the seven elements of the MATCH ME Formula®.

A MATCH ME Formula® Cover Letter

The cover letter addressed to your selectors and submitted in combination with your résumé or CV is intended to introduce you and provide context as to why you are applying and suited for the opportunity. Typically one page, the cover letter should be brief and to the point, with a focus on being memorable and explaining your "why's": *why you, why this opportunity,* and *why now.* A cover letter is commonly used for job applications, but you may also be asked for a cover letter when applying to fellowships and individual grants, awards, and opportunities such as a board position or speaking engagement.

In some cases, a cover letter is made "optional," which might seem like good news if you are trying to save your time and effort. However, I strongly recommend that you not skip the opportunity to submit a cover letter to help you stand out among your competitors. Exceptional candidates are those who go above and beyond and leverage every opportunity to give themselves an edge. Keep in mind, some groups also make cover letters "optional" to assess which candidates are serious and have an authentic desire for the opportunity. So, unless you have a good reason not to include a cover letter, don't skip this step!

Cover Letter Outline The following elements should be included in your cover letter outline:

> **Salutation:** Dear [hiring manager name],
>
> **Introduction (one paragraph):** Your letter introduction should begin with how you align with the organization's mission, which is their approach to solving problems experienced by others. Here, you might also mention if you have been referred by a mutual contact.
>
> **Body (2–5 paragraphs):** In the body of the letter, explain your personal mission and the "why" behind your career steps, such as your choice of college major and degree(s), your current and previous positions, the skills you have gained, and any volunteer experiences that are relevant to the opportunity. In these paragraphs, you are providing evidence that you have an aligned personal mission and will be able to capitalize on two to three of their unique benefits towards advancing their mission. You can express here what you aim to contribute with specific examples.
>
> **Closing (one paragraph):** Express gratitude for the opportunity and include "Thank you for your consideration."

Cover Letter Example In this example, a candidate prepared a cover letter for an Education Analyst role at the Education Policy Research Institute following the MATCH ME framework:

> *Dear Ms. Jones,*
>
> *I am pleased to apply for the Education Analyst role at the Education Policy Research Institute. Professionally and academically, I have been working toward an opportunity to contribute to your mission of*

advancing equal opportunities for all K–12 students. As a first-generation college graduate of immigrant parents, I am particularly interested in applying my skills to the Education Analyst's role of contributing to research and policy initiatives that investigate inequities for immigrant children in public education.

My parents immigrated to the United States from Guatemala in 1995, when I was 4 years old, and they encouraged me to make the most of the public education experiences that I had available to me. With their support, I was able to attend college on merit-based scholarships. After pursuing my undergraduate degree in government at General University, where I graduated with a 3.5 GPA, I have worked at the periphery of education policy, first as a first-grade teacher in New York City public schools through the Teach for America program. In this experience, I offered direct support to child immigrants from Latin American countries who made up approximately 30% of my classroom. To better support these students, many of whom were just beginning to learn English, I leveraged the networks and resources of the TFA program to find a curriculum for English language learners that the children could pursue at home and worked personally with their parents to ensure their commitment to the program. Through this experience, I developed a unique perspective on what it takes from the position of teachers to achieve progress in education equity.

After teaching for two years, I completed my Master in Education at General University, where I prepared my master's thesis on the effectiveness of new English language learning tools in K–12 classrooms. During my studies, I took coursework including Research Methods, Economic Policy Analysis, AI Tools for Social Impact, and Advanced Spanish to develop the skills I needed for education policy research work that I would not be able to find on the job.

Now, as an MEd graduate, I am excited to apply my skills to a professional role in research and policy analysis. The Education Analyst is an excellent next step for me to gain applied qualitative research experience at a junior level and apply new AI tools that I used in my graduate studies. I am motivated to commit to this role because the organization's mission to improve access to education is personal for me. Also, I appreciate how staff at EPRI are encouraged to publish research. I hope to contribute to groundbreaking research that meets the needs of students, families, and EPRI's stakeholders, and gain experience translating and communicating that research to decision makers and the general public through journal publications, white papers, and press releases.

My aim is to help EPRI advance its mission of quality education for all children. I would be honored to be considered for the Education Analyst role. I am happy to provide references who can attest to my skills and work ethic.

Thank you for your consideration.

Sincerely,

This cover letter incorporates the following elements of the MATCH ME Formula®, helping it to stand out among cover letters of other top candidates:

- A **clear personal mission** that is aligned with the organization's mission and goals
- **High detail**, such as mention of the country and year of the parents' immigration, specific master's courses taken, and the attractive aspects of the job description, like preparing journal publications, white papers, and press releases
- A **detailed personal anecdote** of finding and administering a curriculum for immigrant children while at Teach for America, which indicates personal resourcefulness and gives an underlying message of commitment to education

- An explanation of why this person's selection is **mutually beneficial**—they offer a sincere commitment to the organization's mission and authentic desire for the role (backed with evidence)
- A **specific future goal** to contribute to groundbreaking research, which **capitalizes on the organization's unique benefits**
- A tone creating **elegance**, including a note of gratitude: "Thank you for your consideration."

As you prepare cover letters for dream jobs, be sure to do your mission research in advance, identify two to three unique benefits that are not offered elsewhere, and craft a highly specific goal that could be achieved within the same organization.

A MATCH ME *Formula*® *Personal Statement*

A personal statement is a one- to two-page essay that describes your background, future goals, and "why this program." It is commonly required for college and graduate school applications, as well as fellowships, scholarships, and other merit-based awards. Although there can be many different names for this essay, you'll know you are preparing a personal statement if you must respond to questions about your background, motivations, and future goals in an essay format or short-answer responses.

Some of the common questions you are expected to respond to in a personal statement include:

- What is your background?
- Why are you applying to this program?
- What are your academic or career goals?
- How have your personal experiences shaped your interests and goals?

- What is a challenge you have overcome?
- Why are you pursuing this field of study or profession?
- What do you aim to contribute to this field in the future?
- How would your background, identity, and perspective contribute to the diversity of our community?

These are just a few of the most common examples of personal statement prompts, but many programs also include specialty questions, so be sure to look at these closely and consider how you will answer them within the outline provided next. Consider if the specialty questions relate to the story beginning (your background), the middle "hook" (how you will leverage this program for social impact using their unique benefits that you cannot access elsewhere), or the story end (your future goals).

The personal statement is a critical component of your application because in many cases you will not have met the members of the selection committee before. The stakes are high to prepare a creative, easy-to-follow, and attention-grabbing essay that they will remember positively long after reading it. Although there is a creative element to it, the personal statement is not about showing off your creative writing skills; the personal statement is a *tactical document* that answers key questions to help the selection committee make a decision about your selection. The challenge is that you will have a limited word count to answer the many questions they ask. Strong writing skills and creativity are what help this tactical document stand out among the others.

Needless to say, creating an exceptional and memorable personal statement is not easy to do, even for the most skilled writers among us! Writing a great personal statement is a practiced skill that comes from regularly communicating your dreams and values to others in writing and learning how to craft a story from your question responses.

Personal Statement Outline To help guide your practice in crafting a personal statement, you can follow this **5-Part Personal Statement Outline**, using the MATCH ME Formula® as a guidepost for answering personal questions in an essay or short-answer responses. The essay outline has five parts, each representing one to three paragraphs in a specific order, to create an essay of approximately 500–1,000 words.

- **Part 1: A memorable opening story,** which is a personal anecdote that gives an underlying message that you have the characteristics of the organization's ideal candidate
- **Part 2: A summary of your background and motivating influences,** highlighting a few key professional and academic highlights that are relevant to the opportunity
- **Part 3: A highly specific career goal** with a future job title, an example organization, and focused on a specific group or problem you want to help solve with a tangible outcome
- **Part 4: A description of how you will capitalize on two to three of the university's or program's unique benefits,** providing context for why you are applying to this program in particular, creating your application story "hook"
- **Part 5: A closing statement on how you will give back if selected,** demonstrating how your selection is mutually beneficial and expressing gratitude for the opportunity, creating elegance

In addition to the five parts, you should add one **final line of gratitude** to your essay to acknowledge and thank the selector: "Thank you for your consideration."

When you have a personal statement that is limited to one page, or approximately 500 words, each part represents one paragraph. When you are allowed to submit more than 500 words for your personal statement, you can expand some parts of the framework from one to two or more paragraphs. To create the right balance of information that is focused on your future potential in a longer essay, I recommend dedicating a larger portion of your word count to expanding on Part 3, with detail on what you want to achieve in the future, and Part 4, with more detail on the reasons for applying to this particular program.

> **Tip: Your opening story should be very brief and focused and, in some cases, removed.**
>
> Candidates tend to eat up a lot of the word count with their opening story, but keep in mind that the primary goal of the opening story is to grab the reader's attention and prepare them for your coming pitch. The opening story is not as important as the other four parts. In some cases, you may find that a personal opening story is not appropriate for the document, particularly for things like a research proposal, which is primarily about your research plan but may also require responses to questions about your background and career goals.
>
> © Pitch Your Potential / Vicki Johnson, Ph.D.

Personal Statement Example The following is a full personal statement that landed Julie Gardella (introduced in Chapter 2) a spot at the University of Massachusetts–Amherst MBA program with a full-tuition Isenberg Fellowship. Note the application of the 5-Part Personal Statement Outline for a personal statement essay that had a two-page limit (approximately 1,000 words).

I earned my very first dollar picking up pinecones. In my grandfather's front yard grew an enormous pine tree, with long branches that stretched over the grass. My mother offered to pay one penny for every pinecone we picked up, thinking this would be a clever way to clear up the lawn and teach us about the value of earning our money. She figured our short attention spans would amount to just a few pinecones each and that she could probably cover payroll with the spare change in her purse. She was absolutely right about my brother and cousins, who lasted about twenty minutes before they cashed in and ran off to play. Not me. I stayed out there filling bag after bag with pinecones, almost convincing myself that each one was an actual penny. I filled four huge garbage bags of pinecones before I was tired enough to call it quits. When my mom saw how many pinecones I had collected, her eyes widened and her jaw dropped; she could not believe how many I had gathered. She counted out four dollar bills and handed them to me. Four dollars felt like a lot of purchasing power to an eight year old in the early 2000s.

When I entered college a decade later, I channeled that determination into studying climate change and the environment. At NYU, I chose the environmental studies major because I believe that climate change is the most critical issue facing the United States today. My career thus far has not followed a linear path, but my goal is to combine my academic background in sustainability with my professional experience in entrepreneurship. My first full time job after college was at the Harvard Kennedy School of Government's Environment and Natural Resources Program. I organized speaker seminars, oversaw symposium details, and managed our student internship program. I was honored to be part of the driven, dedicated community at Harvard and grateful to meet so many experts at the tops of their fields. I knew that I wanted to pursue a graduate degree, and I realized that I was drawn more to the market deployment of clean energy innovation than to policies driving sustainability.

To gain entrepreneurial experience, I researched and applied to the Alaska Fellows Program (AFP). AFP is a nine-month residential fellowship, where candidates are competitively selected to work at local non-profit or public host organizations in Alaska, and become part of a statewide network of professionals. I chose AFP for its emphasis on professional mentorship, hands-on work experience, and the outdoor opportunities in the unparalleled natural beauty of Alaska. My fellowship host organization was the University of Alaska Center for

Economic Development (UACED), *a university-based start-up ecosystem builder and applied economic research center.*

Choosing UACED as my fellowship host organization was easy because I love entrepreneurship. I love the passion, energy, and excitement around a start-up. As the daughter of a small business owner, I know the hard work, dedication, and resilience it takes to run a company. What I did not know was that it is so much more challenging in Alaska. Alaska is cold, dark, vast, and remote. It has higher shipping, internet, and energy costs than the rest of the country. Its population centers sprawl across hundreds of miles, and many are not connected by road. The entrepreneurs here are the most innovative and resilient people I have ever met, and they have inspired me to further my education in business. After my fellowship year, I transitioned to a full-time position at UACED, honing my applied research skills and taking on more leadership responsibilities in our entrepreneurship programming. This experience further invigorated my passion for innovation and drive to pursue my education in business that will lead to a top position at an innovative company with a mission to combat climate change.

The Isenberg MBA program's rigorous quantitative curriculum, flexible elective courses, and access to exceptional start-up resources like the Berthiaume Center for Entrepreneurship will equip me with the tools and network I need to combine my multidisciplinary background with my career goals. Moreover, the Isenberg Fellowship removes the barrier of financing the enormous cost of graduate school, allowing students to prioritize their coursework, campus involvement, and professional development instead of making ends meet. As an undergraduate, I worked long hours, often in service jobs that did not support my career goals to cover tuition and basic living expenses. With the Isenberg MBA, I am confident I can spend my time working on what matters to me: building my analytical skills, getting involved in campus groups, expanding my peer network, and finding mentorship with UMass's exceptional faculty. After graduating close to debt free, the Isenberg MBA will empower me to choose my dream job at an exciting start-up without financial restraints.

While pursuing my degree, I intend to combine my multifaceted professional experience with my academic background to contribute to the Isenberg School's research output and reputation as a leading public business program. An experienced researcher, I possess a strong intellectual curiosity and deep commitment to accessibility of information that I am eager to further develop while in graduate school. For example, I designed and conducted a research case study on a business plan competition in a rural region of Western Alaska. My report became an important reference for the program's new director and provided supporting documentation for federal grant funding for the program. Lastly, it was adapted into an article in the Alaska Journal of Commerce as part of a Techstars Startup Week series. I have honed my ability to combine data-driven methodology with empathetic qualitative information to develop informative, accessible research that engages a wide audience. I hope to contribute my experience and dedication to the Isenberg School's academic research output, while gaining mentorship from its leading faculty to advance knowledge and make a positive impact on the business community.

At UMass, I hope to build connections with the distinguished faculty, my fellow classmates, and the vast alumni network of the Isenberg School to help me achieve my goals. My experience as an Alaska Fellow has really highlighted for me the importance of a strong, genuine professional network; I continue to give my time to AFP events, actively welcome new Fellows to Alaska, and volunteer annually on its alumni career panel. Fostering a network like this during my graduate studies at UMass Amherst is a priority for me because as a business leader, being part of a community of innovative, like-minded colleagues and mentors opens opportunities for collaboration on future projects and broadens access to multidisciplinary expertise. Lastly, I am the happiest and most driven person I can be when I have spent time in nature hiking, biking, kayaking, or camping. Amherst offers all these in the backyard of its vibrant community with all the amenities of a small city. I would be thrilled to study in Amherst and am committed to helping build its thriving and equitable start-up ecosystem for years to come.

Thank you for your time and consideration.

The following MATCH ME Formula® elements helped Julie's statement stand out among those of other top candidates:

- **An opening personal anecdote with high detail** (one paragraph), making it memorable and demonstrating that Julie has the characteristics of their ideal candidate, including personal drive and an entrepreneurial mindset
- **Detail about her background, with a few key career highlights, and her career goal** (three paragraphs), helping explain the career pathway outlined in her accompanying résumé and why she wants to attend graduate school at this point in her career; she ends with her career goal to "lead to a top position at an innovative company with a mission to combat climate change"
- **How she will capitalize on the Isenberg MBA's unique benefits** (two paragraphs), including the Berthiaume Center for Entrepreneurship, the school's focus on research, and the full-tuition funding offered by the Isenberg Fellowship for incoming students
- **How her selection is mutually beneficial** (one paragraph) because of the community engagement she will offer, stating how she will "build connections with the distinguished faculty, my fellow classmates, and the vast alumni network," helping to make a long-term social impact on the university community

She also included one **final line of gratitude** to show elegance: "Thank you for your time and consideration."

As you can see, Julie followed the 5-Part Personal Statement Outline but made it her own through the high level of detail she added to each paragraph. She was careful to balance future-facing information with her background information, painting a compelling vision of her future potential and contribution that landed her an acceptance.

MATCH ME Formula® Interview Prep

Most competitive opportunities have an interview component, where you answer questions live with an individual or panel of people. Never "wing" an interview for a dream job, award, or elite opportunity. Use the following tips to ensure you make a strong, positive impression that you are a great fit for the opportunity.

Interview Prep Steps Follow these steps to help you prepare for an interview and ensure that your interview presentation and responses reflect your application story and the seven elements of the MATCH ME Formula®.

> **Step 1: Create your application story.** Your story will serve as a centering piece when you are responding to questions. This helps ensure your message to selectors is consistent and powerful. Being consistent in your responses demonstrates your authentic desire for the role; likewise, inconsistent responses signal you are not a serious candidate. When you get stumped with a question, you can refer mentally to the components of your application story to help craft a powerful response:
>
> **The beginning:** Your background up until this point
> **The end:** The achievement of your highly specific and timely future goal, which fulfills your personal mission and the organization's mission

The middle "hook": How the organization offers specific, unique benefits that you will capitalize on to achieve your future goal while advancing their mission

You should know your application story cold before going into an interview. Your application story might be different for each opportunity you apply to (and if the opportunities are wide-ranging, they should be!). So, if you are applying for and interviewing for several jobs, universities, or award programs at once, be sure to refer to the application story that you devised for the initial application.

Step 2: Create a list of possible interview questions. Consider which questions you are likely to be asked in the interview and prepare a list of examples from your experiences that you can use in your responses. Using an AI tool, you can create a list of questions that reflect the job requirements and expectations, as well as commonly asked interview questions. When possible, connect with current and former employees, students, and winners of the organization to ask what questions you might be asked in the interview. Often, you will need to answer questions that demonstrate:

- Your expertise
- Challenges you've overcome: professional, academic, and personal
- How you approach complex problems
- How you contribute to teams
- How you juggle multiple tasks and meet deadlines
- Your innovative ideas
- Your leadership experience *(for leadership opportunities)*
- Your people management experience *(for management opportunities)*
- Your research skills *(for academic opportunities)*

Step 3: Create a "treasure chest" of examples. You want to have mentally on hand a list of highly specific examples of your accomplishments, approaches, challenges overcome, and areas of expertise—what I call a "treasure chest." Specific examples are what make your interview responses powerful and compelling. People who don't prepare for interviews may struggle to recall important examples when put on the spot. You want to create a list and reflect on it several times, especially in the hour before your interview, to help with memory recall. Being able to respond to questions with specific examples will help you to feel more confident and in control and will make a great impression on selectors. When possible, have a brief one-page list of your "treasure chest" examples from your experiences nearby—for example, next to your computer if you are doing an online interview or in a notebook you hold in your lap if you are doing an in-person interview.

Interview Prep Example Imagine you are a midcareer professional who has worked for 15 years in philanthropic fundraising for a large national nonprofit in environmental conservation and you are about to interview for a dream role to become Vice President of Philanthropic Advising for Tall Trees Alliance, a national professional association that provides specialized services to help climate philanthropists. The role involves directly engaging high-net-worth individuals and families, providing strategic guidance to foster transformative and scalable philanthropy, and managing a team of 10 people.

Using this example, here are the steps you would take to prepare for the interview:

Step 1: Create your application story. Here is an example of what your application story might look like:

Your Background: *For the past 15 years, I've led philanthropic fundraising initiatives at the national level for one of the largest*

U.S.-based nonprofits dedicated to environmental conservation. In that role, I built long-standing partnerships with major donors and family foundations, helping to raise more than $200 million to support climate resilience, land preservation, and biodiversity initiatives across the country. I've also led cross-functional teams and developed donor education programs that helped philanthropists align their giving with high-impact, science-based strategies. Before this I worked in other philanthropic roles and earned my bachelor's in earth sciences and my master in public policy.

Your Future Goals: *At this stage in my career, I want to shift from traditional fundraising to a more advisory and strategic role, helping donors not just give more but give more effectively. I'm especially interested in scaling philanthropy that supports systems change, such as climate justice, clean energy innovation, and Indigenous land stewardship. I would like to help Tall Trees Alliance reach its goal to implement solar and wind energy projects in more than 30 economically disadvantaged U.S. districts.*

Why This Opportunity (The "Hook"): *Your mission to support climate philanthropists with strategic tools and guidance directly aligns with how I want to spend the next chapter of my career: coaching, advising, and scaling the impact of individuals and families. I'm also excited by the chance to lead and mentor a team of experts so we can amplify the most effective climate solutions that are facing political resistance and need more exposure and support.*

Step 2: Create a list of possible interview questions. Using the job description and your mission research of the organization, identify possible interview questions you must prepare for. Here are categories of questions you would identify for this particular example:

Your Expertise and Personal Philosophy: To assess how you think and operate, the organization might ask questions

that probe your expertise and how you would approach specific job tasks. Questions might include:
- *How do you define "transformational philanthropy," and how have you helped donors achieve it in your past work?*
- *What trends are you seeing in climate philanthropy, and how would you help our donors respond to those trends strategically?*

Leadership and Management Experience: To assess the type of leader and manager you will be, they might ask about your past experiences. Questions might include:
- *Tell us about a time you led a team through a major strategic shift or organizational change. What was your approach?*
- *How do you build and manage a high-performing team of advisors or fundraisers, especially when they bring diverse styles and expertise?*
- *What role do you think mentorship plays in this work, and how do you support professional growth among your staff?*

Your Innovative Ideas: To assess if you have vision and drive and can execute projects, they might ask you to provide examples of ideas that you were responsible for implementing. Questions might include:
- *Can you share an example of a donor relationship that evolved into a multiyear, high-impact partnership? What made it successful?*
- *How do you approach advising high-net-worth individuals and families who are newer to climate philanthropy?*

Your Motivations and Personal Goals: All selectors want to choose people who are mission-aligned and have ambitious personal goals. Questions might include:
- *Why is this the right time for you to move from a fundraising role into a philanthropic advising role?*
- *What would success look like for you in this role after the first 12 months?*

These are just a few examples! Be sure to brainstorm all possible questions.

Step 3: Create a "treasure chest" of examples. Once you have a list of possible questions, it's time to brainstorm examples from your experience that could help answer these questions. Brainstorm not just what you did but *how* you did it: this is the most important detail to include. Think of ways that you effectively gathered resources, problem-solved, and achieved buy-in. Also consider outcomes: think beyond the thing that was created, such as the product, service, or policy, and consider how the outcome positively impacted others in the immediate and long term. From this brainstorm, identify three to five examples from your experience that you can speak on in-depth that exhibit your expertise and resourcefulness, your leadership and management skills, your innovative ideas, and your motivations and future goals. These examples make up your "treasure chest."

 **Tip: Don't attempt to memorize your interview responses.**

Memorized responses can come off as stilted and inauthentic. Instead, keep your bullets nearby (or ideally, in your mind) and practice speaking about these examples in a mock interview with a mentor or friend. The more you practice discussing examples of your experience in detail, the easier it will be to respond to interview questions smoothly and without notes.

© Pitch Your Potential / Vicki Johnson, Ph.D.

Guiding Questions to Apply the MATCH ME Formula®

Once you create the drafts of your application components and prepare for interviews, use these guiding questions to determine if you have fully applied the MATCH ME Formula® in your application story and responses. I recommend asking your mentors who review your applications for feedback to also use these guiding questions to help you find gaps in your application (which can be difficult to see after you've read your draft many times!).

1. Have I found a way to be **memorable** to selectors, through a referral, a self-introduction, and/or detailed personal anecdotes, career goals, and ideas in my application?
2. Do I explicitly say how my personal mission **aligns** with the organization's mission?
3. Are my proposed ideas **timely**, meaning they address the organization's priority challenges and goals now and within the next 12 months? Have I expressed urgency in my application by giving them a reason why I need this opportunity now and not later?
4. Have I identified the unique benefits, resources, people, or experiences that are only available to me through this opportunity, and have I expressed how I will **capitalize** on two to three of these unique benefits if I am selected?
5. Am I **highly specific** in each sentence of my application by including:
   a. Detail in my personal anecdotes that helps the reader visualize the scene in their own mind and recall my stories to others?
   b. Detail in my personal mission and career goals that helps the reader visualize me in a specific role in the future?
   c. Detail in my proposed ideas for helping the organization achieve its mission?

d. Detail in describing two to three of their unique benefits that I will capitalize on?
6. Have I demonstrated that my selection is **mutually beneficial** by expressing how my selection will benefit the organization's mission and also benefit me in gaining resources, skills, networks, and experiences I need to achieve my personal mission and goals?
7. Is my application **elegant** by having a balanced tone of self-confidence and humility and expressing gratitude to the selectors for their consideration?

We Believe in You

You have everything you need to achieve your dreams. Create a blueprint that maps out where you are now to where you want to be in the future, and follow that blueprint one step at a time using the MATCH ME Formula®.

> Remember: **You deserve the opportunities to access the education, resources, experiences, and networks you need to make the greatest social impact possible with your unique set of talents, perspectives, and skills.**

Even at times when you lack a guide or encouraging support, know that the ProFellow community and I are rooting for your success every step of the way.

References

Accenture. 2025. "Accenture's What We Do - Capabilities." Retrieved May 29. https://www.accenture.com/us-en/services.

Authority Magazine. 2020. "CJ Isakow: 5 Things I Wish Someone Told Me Before I Became CEO of Eyebloc." July 27. https://medium.com/authority-magazine/cj-isakow-5-things-i-wish-someone-told-me-before-i-became-ceo-of-eyebloc-6e07a75ae227.

Berman, Jeff. 2024. "How The Flex Company Disrupted Menstrual Care (with Founder & CEO Lauren Wang)." Podcast interview. Posted December 5, 2024, by Masters of Scale. YouTube, 35:01. https://youtu.be/TyWfYpq4h5k.

Broe, Palle. 2025. "Pulling back the curtain on the magic of Y Combinator." *Lenny's Newsletter*, February 11. https://www.lennysnewsletter.com/p/pulling-back-the-curtain-on-the-magic.

Cass, Shawna. 2022. "Frank A. Burtner award winner goes above and beyond for students." *Clemson News*, May 31. https://news.clemson.edu/2022-frank-a-burtner-award-winner-robyn-curtis.

Forbes. 2025. "Who We Are." Forbes - Connect with Us. Effective May 28. https://www.forbes.com/connect/who-we-are/.

Ford, Jim Burke. 2025. "Reasons to Choose Ford over the Competition." Effective May 28. https://www.jimburkeford.com/reasons-to-choose-ford-over-the-competition/.

Gates Foundation. 2025. "About." Effective May 28. https://www.gatesfoundation.org/about.

Glassdoor Team. 2015. "50 HR & Recruiting Stats That Make You Think." https://www.glassdoor.com/blog/50-hr-recruiting-stats-make-think/.

Goleman, Daniel. 2005. *Emotional Intelligence: Why It May Matter More than IQ.* Bantam.

Jiang, Jia. 2016. "What I learned from 100 days of rejection." December 7. Presented at TEDxMtHood. https://youtu.be/-vZXgApsPCQ.

John, Daymond. 2025. "Behind the Scenes of Shark Tank as a Startup." Effective May 28. https://daymondjohn.com/blogs/journal/84017860-behind-the-scenes-of-shark-tank-as-a-startup.

Knox, Liam. 2023. "Graduate Applications Up, but Enrollment Falls." *Inside Higher Ed*, October 18. https://www.insidehighered.com/news/admissions/graduate/2023/10/18/graduate-enrollment-slows-even-applications-surge.

Kueppers, Courtney. 2016. "Fulbright Seeks More Diverse Pool of Scholars and Students." The Chronicle of Higher Ed, February 22. https://www.chronicle.com/article/fulbright-seeks-more-diverse-pool-of-scholars-and-students/.

Mata, Elainy. 2022. "How to Write a Cover Letter That Sounds Like You (and Gets Noticed)." Harvard Business Review, May 10. https://hbr.org/2022/05/how-to-write-a-cover-letter-that-sounds-like-you-and-gets-noticed.

Mowreader, Ashley. 2024 "Campus Engagement Tip: Promoting Athletic Event Attendance." *Inside Higher Ed*, September 5. https://www.insidehighered.com/news/student-success/college-experience/2024/09/05/seven-ways-promote-school-spirit-and-college.

Mox, Kyle. 2019. "Exposing the black market of fellowship advising." *University Business*, October 21. https://universitybusiness.com/exposing-the-black-market-of-fellowship-advising/.

NYC.gov. 2025. "New York City Urban Fellows." NYC DCAS Citywide Adminstrative Services, June 16. https://www.nyc.gov/site/dcas/employment/internship-and-fellowships-nyc-urban-fellows.page.

Obama, Michelle. 2018. *Becoming*. New York: Crown Publishing Group.

Parker, Victoria. 2022. "Studying Abroad While Black: Examining Study Abroad from the Perspective of Black Students at Historically Black Colleges and Universities." CMSI Research Brief, Rutgers University. https://cmsi.gse.rutgers.edu/sites/default/files/Studying%20Abroad%20While%20Black%202022.pdf.

ProFellow. 2025. "About Us." Effective August 15. https://www.profellow.com/about-us/.

Quantic. 2022. "How to Get a Job at Google." *Quantic – Career Planning*, October 28. https://quantic.edu/blog/2022/10/28/how-to-get-a-job-at-google/.

Robinson, Brian. 2024. "Why 80% of Hiring Managers Discard AI-Generated Job Applications from Career Seekers." *Forbes*, October 20. https://www.forbes.com/sites/bryanrobinson/2024/10/20/why-80-of-hiring-managers-discard-ai-generated-job-applications-from-career-seekers/.

Schisgall, Elias J. and Shah, Neil H. 2023. "A Bigger Harvard? Rethinking Access in 'Elite' Higher Education." *The Harvard Crimson*, November 16. https://www.thecrimson.com/article/2023/11/16/class-size-scrut/.

Semuels, Alana. 2023. "You're Not Imagining It—Job Hunting Is Getting Worse." *Time*, June 14. https://time.com/6287012/why-finding-job-is-difficult/.

Tesla. 2025. "About Us." Effective May 28. https://www.tesla.com/about.

U.S. Department of Education. 2025. "Mission of the U.S. Department of Education." Page last reviewed January 14, 2025. Effective

May 28. https://www.ed.gov/about/ed-overview/mission-of-the-us-department-of-education.

William & Mary. 2025. "Majors & Minors: History." Effective August 15. https://www.wm.edu/majorsminors/history/.

Wu, Natalie. 2024. "How Raising Cane's Founder Todd Graves Became an Unlikely Billionaire." *CNBC*, October 5. https://www.cnbc.com/2024/10/05/how-raising-canes-founder-todd-graves-became-unlikely-billionaire.html.

Y Combinator. 2025. "Y Combinator: Make Something People Want." Effective May 28. https://www.ycombinator.com/.

Work with Me

ProFellow's motto is "Do something exceptional." I invite you to join the ProFellow movement to make opportunities more accessible and advance your career through the pursuit of professional and academic fellowships, graduate study, business accelerators, and other elite opportunities. There are several ways you can join the ProFellow community and collaborate with me.

Individuals

I invite you to create a free account at ProFellow.com to access our comprehensive database of fellowships, awards, business accelerators, and graduate study opportunities. At ProFellow, you can also join our popular mailing list, access high-quality articles written by award winners, and join events and workshops that help you develop a competitive application.

You can also visit my personal website at www.DrVickiJohnson.com to learn about my latest offerings and book individual advising, including executive coaching, graduate admissions coaching, and mentorship sessions.

Organizations

If you are seeking a dynamic speaker on topics including the winner's mindset, overcoming invisible barriers, and developing a compelling personal pitch, book me for a keynote, seminar, or workshop for your team or conference at www.DrVickiJohnson.com.

Acknowledgments

I could not have written this book without the support of the thousands of people who comprise my network, including my family, friends, professional and academic mentors, colleagues, and members of the wider ProFellow community, who inspire me daily to engage in this work.

First and foremost, I must thank my best friend and husband, Ryan, who has served as an unconditional source of support for my career and personal aspirations since our first date. It was Ryan who conceived the idea to create ProFellow® and provide the world with a website about fellowships and graduate funding. Ryan is one of those unique risk-takers whose optimism is boundless and contagious. Ryan saw my potential as an entrepreneur, writer, speaker, and leader, and supported my path every step of the way, including taking on family and financial responsibilities as we have moved and lived in four different places, raised our two children, and committed to growing a company that first and foremost would remain true to our values. Although he has always been just as committed to the ProFellow idea as I have, he takes none of the spotlight, quietly serving as the operational, technical, and emotional support system that powers ProFellow. His unwavering support gave me everything I needed to write and publish this book. Ryan, I can't thank you enough for being the husband, father, friend, and support system that has allowed me to pursue my dreams and our life's adventures. I love you.

Thank you, Penn and Liv, for giving me endless hugs and high-fives while I wrote in my office/playroom filled with toys, craft projects, and all forms of mess that make me smile. I will look back on these days fondly.

I would like to thank my parents, who planted the seeds for my success by raising me and teaching me resilience, patience, and love. Your service to others is the service I strive to emulate. I hope to make you both proud.

Thank you to my acquisition editor, Leah Zarra, who saw my potential from our first conversation and brought this book to life. I also thank my developmental editor, Angela Morrison, who provided me with the expertise I needed to succeed while also cultivating my confidence, as a true guide does.

I would like to thank those who participated in an interview with me and generously shared their application materials to be featured in the book, including Camille Serrano, Craig Isakow, Erin Gallagher, Jack Sullivan, Jamaal Glenn, Julie Gardella, Dr. Kate Golebiowska, Kristina McLaughlin, Mona Sabet, Oumama Kabli, Rachel Santarsiero, and Sojourner White.

I would like to thank the thousands of supporters and longtime members of the ProFellow community, including our institutional partners and their leaders, who have been instrumental in ProFellow's success. I appreciate the support of each and every one of you.

I'd like to send gratitude to my Ph.D. advisor and mentor, the late Dr. David Johnston (1966–2025), a Distinguished Professor at Massey University and Director of the Joint Centre for Disaster Research in New Zealand. I will never forget his support, sense of humor, and aspirational thinking, which inspired me to think bigger and not give up. His mentorship had a profound influence on how I mentor others today, ensuring his legacy endures. *Whakawhetai ki a koe*, David.

Finally, I give one last shout-out to the Wilmington High School class of 1997 and my band, theater, and field hockey friends. You are deeply rooted in the fabric of who I am today.

About the Author

Dr. Vicki Johnson is a speaker, author, and four-time fellowship winner who helps ambitious professionals achieve elite opportunities. She is the founder of ProFellow®, the leading U.S. platform for competitive fellowships, graduate programs, and leadership accelerators, read by more than nine million people globally. As a sought-after speaker and coach, Vicki teaches storytelling strategies that have helped ProFellow members secure more than $500 million in merit-based funding awards. *Pitch Your Potential* is her first book and serves as an in-depth guide to her breakthrough MATCH ME Formula®, representing the seven elements of a winning application. Vicki invites you to connect with her at www.DrVickiJohnson.com.

Index

A
academia, 24, 62, 126
Accenture, 128
acceptance rate, 3, 7, 35, 36, 50, 100, 147
accomplishment, 7, 8, 23, 41, 64, 102, 103, 111, 116, 125, 127, 140, 141, 167, 170, 173, 175, 176
achievement, 6, 9, 12, 22, 27, 30, 65, 127, 175
Adidas, 103
advisors, 13, 14
Alaska Fellows Program (AFP), 196
Alexander von Humboldt Foundation, 89
alignment, 4, 7, 23, 29, 58, 59, 72–73, 76–81, 111, 116, 126, 131, 136, 139, 168, 183, 187
  application story, 187

career goal, 60
mission, 61–64, 76, 77, 79, 80, 102, 183
  in pitch, 61
ambition, 6, 15, 16, 19, 27
  personal, 60, 64, 65, 79
AmeriCorps VISTA, 166
anecdote
  in cover letter, 54
  memorable, 26, 51–52
  negative, 52
  personal, 37, 38
application
  jargon in, 126
  urgency and timeliness, 95
application story, 7, 26–27, 184, 206
  alignment, 187
  beginning, 185
  capitalize, 187
  elegance, 187
  end, 185

application story (*continued*)
  "hero" of, 110–111
  highly specific, 187
  MATCH ME Formula®, 206
  memorable, 187
  middle, 185
  mutually beneficial, 187
  selectors' question, 26
  timely, 187
  winning, 184
apprenticeship, 57
artificial intelligence (AI)
  generated résumés, 36
  tools, 25, 36, 105, 117
Ashoka Fellows, 103
attendance, 2, 20, 43, 44
attention, 19, 34–36, 38, 39
authentic desire, 7, 60, 101, 112, 183
  advantage of, 23–25
awards, 64, 104, 113, 136, 150, 151

B

Bardack, Stephanie, 120
Becoming (Obama 2018), 15, 16
benefits
  educational, needs for, 157–158
  financial, needs for, 153
  network, needs for, 158–161
  paying forward, 161–164
  unique, 101–102, 116–118

Ben Griffen experiment, 44
Bill & Melinda Gates Foundation, 67
Bradley University, 49
business accelerator, 64, 158
business card, 45

C

Capital Area Food Network, 166
capitalize, 101, 183, 187, 192
  unique benefits, 101–102, 113–118
career
  advice, 1, 7
  alignment goal, 60
  change, 71, 158
  competitions of, 23
  definition, 135
  goal, 24, 129–131, 155
  opportunities, 163
  in public service, 155
  tracks, 136
ChatGPT, 35, 105, 117
chief marketing officer (CMO), 17
Churchill, Sarah, 78
Churchill, Winston, 78
Civil Rights Movement, 2
cold pitch by email, 33, 34
communication, 11, 41, 109, 170
  persuasive, xiii, 26
  to selectors, 178
  skills, 8, 49

comparison
  fear of, 19–21
  psychology of, 21
comparison culture, 19,
  22, 172, 176
competition, xi, 1, 2, 4, 5, 7, 8,
  10, 11, 13, 20–26, 29, 58,
  68, 95, 100, 125, 172,
  179, 181, 182
competitive programs and
  awards, 151
competitor differentiators, 68, 81
confidence, 21, 39, 122, 130,
  172, 179, 183
  career with, 2
  in pitch, 30
Cornell University, 2, 41
  acceptance letter, 6
  campus, 3
  selection committee, 5–6
Council of Graduate Schools, 36
courage, 9, 18, 183
cover letter, 25, 66, 102, 121, 125
  AI-generated, 36
  anecdote in, 54
  body, 189
  career goal, 131
  clear personal mission, 191
  closing, 189
  detailed personal anecdote, 191
  for Education Analyst
    role, 189–191
  elegance, 192

high detail, 191
introduction, 189
MATCH ME
  Formula®, 188–189
memorable, 54
mutually beneficial, 192
outline, 189–191
salutation, 189
specific future goal, 192
specificity, 127–128
writing, 25–26
creative, 34
Curtis, Robyn, 17, 18
Custer, Daniel, 17, 18

D

Damian, 130, 131
The Daughters of Yalta, 78
decision-making, 21,
  114, 156, 170
  selection committee's, 5
Department of Health and
  Human Services
  (HHS), 120
Department of Health and
  Mental Hygiene
  (DOHMH), 90
desire, 9, 20, 22–25, 30, 59, 60,
  64, 65, 74, 94, 167
  authentic, 7, 23–25, 60,
    101, 112, 183
digital documentation, 39,
  42–43

Disaster Research Center, 91
discouragement, 7, 12–14, 16, 30, 58, 175, 182
discrimination, 14, 151
  forms of, 10
Dombrowsky, Wolf, 91

E
Echoing Green, 103
educational benefits, needs for, 157–158
effort, xiv, 5, 9–12, 14, 16, 17, 21–24, 30, 61, 64, 65, 79, 90, 93, 96, 108, 142, 147, 149, 162, 171, 172, 176, 177, 182–184, 186, 188
  unrewarded, 14
Einhorn Center, 42
elegance, 124, 187, 192, 194, 199
  definition, 169
  self-confidence, 173
  winner's mindset, 171–173
embarrassment, 21
Emory University, 138
emotional intelligence (EQ), 169–171, 179
Emotional Intelligence: Why It May Matter More Than IQ, 169
empathy, for selectors, 177
encouragement, 13
essay, 194
expectations *vs.* goals, 7
Eyebloc, 98, 99

F
failure, 16, 19, 21, 22, 30, 99, 171
  discrimination, 10
  emotional pain, 9
  fear of, 8–12
  as opportunities, 10
  reflection, 10–11
  and rejection, 8–12
  and success, 10
fear, 30, 171, 172
  of comparison, 19–21
  of failure, 8–12
feedback, 1–3, 9, 13, 15, 18
  constructive, 21
  from mentor, 102
  positive, 41
fellowships, 63–64, 136, 157, 188, 192
  organizations mission, 63–64
financial benefits, 155
  needs for, 153
Fisch, Allan, 99–101
Flex Company, 17
Forbes, 67
Ford, Jim Burke, 68
Ford Motor Company, 68
Foreign Service, 145
Foreign Service Officer (FSO), 88, 145
Foreign Service Officer Test (FSOT), 145

Frank A. Burtner Award for Excellence in Advising, 18
Fulbright award, xv, 77
   English Teaching Assistantship (ETA) Award, 50, 147
   U.S. Student Award program, 49
   Visiting Scholar Award, 138–139

G

Gallagher, Erin, 165
Gallo, Amy, 54
Gardella, Julie, 52, 53, 195
gatekeepers, 182
   failure and messaging from, 19–21
   impact of, 12
   vs. listen to guides, 16–18
gatekeeping, 12
   deliberate, 12–14
   types of, 12
   well-intentioned, 14–16
generative AI writing tools, 25
George Mason University (GMU), 146
German Chancellor Fellowship, xiii, 89–91
Ginsburg, Ruth Bader, 4
Girl Scout Gold Award, 4
Glenn, Jamaal, 160–161
Global food security, 167

GMC, 68
goals
   career, 129–130
   vs. expectations, 7
   highly specific, 123
   leadership team, 72
   mission statements and, 67
   personal, 7
   supplementary, 71
   timely, 83–96 (*see also* timeliness)
Golebiowska, Kate, 138
Goleman, Daniel, 169
Google, 35
GPA, 13, 23, 58, 61, 62, 81, 167, 190
grants, 136
gratitude, 178, 199
Graves, Todd, 15
Greenpeace, 103
grit, 16, 146, 183
guides, 16–18, 142
   listening to, 16–18

H

Harriman, Kathleen, 78
Harvard Business Review (HBR) article, 54
Harvard College, 36
Harvard Law School, 16
Harvard University, 103
higher education industry, 69
HiPower, 33

"hook" story, 26, 27, 31, 101, 110, 117, 131, 185, 186, 193, 194, 201, 203
humility, 168, 169, 173, 179

I
idea proposal, 48–49
  creative and memorable, 49
impostor syndrome, 16, 175, 176
incentives, 14
Inside Higher Education, 43
internship, 40, 58–60, 83, 84, 116, 132, 159
  government, 58
interview
  application story, 202–203
  examples, 205
  innovative ideas, 204
  leadership and management experience, 204
  MATCH ME Formula®, 200–205
  motivations and personal goals, 204
  possible interview questions, 201–204
  prep, 200–203
  skills, 80
  steps, 200
  thank you email, 108–110
interviewer, 129
introductions, 54

  from influential mutual contact, 42
  positive response, 40–41
  question preparations, 41
  to selector, 40–41
investigative research, 76
  as skill, 8
investors, 29, 40, 64
Isakow, Craig, 97–98, 101
Isenberg Fellowship, 52
Ivy League university, 2, 4

J
jargon, 123
  in application, 126
  replace, 125–126
  specific, 127–128
  vague, 127–128
Jiang, Jia, 9
job, 157
  competition for, 35
  entry-level, 166
  permanent, 156
Johns Hopkins School of Advanced International Studies (SAIS), 149
Johnston, David, 216

K
Kabli, Oumama, 145, 146, 148–150
Kam, Cindy, 44
Katz, Catherine Grace, 78
Kwanzaa principles, 50, 51

L

leadership, 6
   team goals, 72
leadership position
   capitalize and, 106
   opportunities, 10
   recruitment, 113
legacy, 4, 6, 73, 162, 217
LinkedIn.com, 35, 39
   for mutual and self-introductions, 42–43
   network of contacts on, 42
   selector connection in, 48

M

Marshall Memorial Fellowship (MMF), 161
Masters of Scale podcast, 17
Mata, Elainy, 54
MATCH ME Formula®, xviii, 2, 61, 85, 93, 101, 116, 121, 123, 147, 149, 150, 166, 167, 169, 181, 183
   alignment, 61
   application story, 28–31, 206
   capitalize, 101, 116 (*see also* capitalize)
   career goal, 130–134
   cover letter, 188–189
   elegant, 169
   elements of, 8
   frameworks, 187–188
   guiding questions, 206–207
   highly specific, 123
   interview prep, 200–205
   memorability, 34–35
   personal statement, 192–200
   seven key elements, 8, 28
   timeliness (*see* timeliness)
McKinsey, 98
memorability, 35–37
   anecdote in cover letter, 54
   detailed, 37
   five factors of, 48
   idea proposal, 48–49
   meaningful, 37–38
   novel, 37
   personal, 38
   personal anecdote usage, 51–52
   positive, 35, 37–56
   with practice, 54–55
   "stickiness," 34
   strategies, 39
mental barrier, 12
mentors, 142
merit-based funding, 111, 115, 153, 190, 192
"midcareer" leadership program, 71
"midlife crisis," 24
mindset, 167, 169
   and tactical strategies, 181
   winner's (*see* winner's mindset)

mission
  alignment, 61–64, 76–80, 102, 183
  companies, 63
  demonstration, 65–67
  organization, 63–64
  research on, 66–67
  search online for, 81
  statements, 67
  statements and goals, 67
  work experience and accolades, 62
money, 154, 156
Moonshot Brands, 100
Mox, Kyle, 13
mutual benefit, 150

N

Nasdaq Entrepreneurial Center's Milestone Makers program, xvi
National Association of County and City Health Officials, 121
National Churchill Library Center (NCLC), 77
National Commission on Children and Disasters, 119
National Science Foundation fellowship, 17
Nature Conservancy, 103
needs
  definition, 153
  for educational benefits, 157–158
  financial, 155
  for financial benefits, 153
  for network benefits, 158–161
  personal, 152–153
  self-centric, 65
negotiation, 25, 26, 129, 143, 145, 157
  as skill, 8
negotiator, 129
network benefits
  needs for, 158–161
  in pitch, 160–161
New York City government, 60
New York City Urban Fellows Program, 57–60, 74, 89
  eligibility, 59
  mission of, 60
New York University, 52
Nike, 103
nonprofit and government organizations, 63
Northern Virginia Community College, 146
numbers game, 22–23, 125

O

Obama, Michelle, 15–16
offer decline, 112–113
"one-click" application, 35
On-Site Volunteer Services, 60
opportunity, 10, 11, 80, 81, 85

career, 163
cohort-based, 81, 85
competitive, 22, 93
mission alignment, 61–64
mutual benefit, 151
organization's unique
  benefits, 118
selective, 23
success and failure as, 10
unique benefits of, 104
optimism, 22
optimist, 168
organization
  capitalize on, 106–110
  mission, 63–64, 80
  opportunity, 104
  press releases and news
    features, 69–70
  unique benefits, 104, 113–118
  website, 86, 105
overconfident, 172, 174

P

pandemic, 120
partnerships, 105
Pell Grant, 153
personal ambition, 79
personal mission, 73–76
  clear cover letter, 191
  definition, 73
personal needs, 152–153
personal pitch, 25–26
personal statement, 58, 115

MATCH ME
  Formula®, 192–200
  opening story, 195
  outline, 193–195
  written memorable, 55
persuasive writing
  as skill, 8
philanthropy, 72
pitch, 2, 7
  confidence in, 30
  network benefits in, 160–161
  personal, 25–26
  persuasive, 25
  sales, 34
  unique benefits in, 102
  urgency in, 93–96
platitudes, 125–126
  in application, 126
  specific, 127–128
  vague, 127–128
policy director role, 120
positive memorability
  detailed, 37
  five factors of, 37–56
  meaningful, 37–38
  novel, 37
  personal, 38
  "stickiness," 38
post-interview "thank you"
  email, 108–110
press releases and news
  features, 105
Princeton University, 15

procrastination, 10, 21
ProFellow®, 7, 28, 68, 77, 93,
    123, 163, 213
  community, 208
  definition, 68
  founders, 28
  opportunities on, 151
professional title, 120
project proposal
  specific, 138–139
  timeliness, 89–91
proposal
  specific project, 138–139
  timeliness, 89–91
  written memorable, 55
public health preparedness, 90
Public Utilities Commission
    (PUC), 108

R
racism, 50
Raising Cane's Chicken
    Fingers, 15
recommendation letter,
    58, 140, 141
referees, 140–142
reference, 11, 40, 41, 46, 84, 140
  external, 141
  specific, 140–142
referral, 36, 121
  for awards and fellowships, 40
  direct, 39
  effective, 40

for graduate programs, 40
for investors and business
    accelerators, 40
for job/internship, 40
from mutual contact, 39–43
offline applications through, 36
request, 41
to selectors, 40–41
rejection, 177
  discrimination, 10
  emotional fear of, 11
  emotional pain, 9
  fear of, 8–11
  reflection, 10–11
Reno, Janet, 4
reputation, 12, 55, 72, 76, 118
research, 29, 41, 44, 47–50, 58,
    59, 61, 63, 69–73, 76–81,
    84–88, 92, 102–105, 115,
    118, 120, 121, 126,
    130–132, 137, 139, 148,
    155, 158, 159, 166, 186,
    189–191, 196–199
  investigative, 8
  organization's mission,
    66–67
resilience, 16, 197, 203, 216
résumé, 13, 25, 58
  of achievement, 22
  AI-generated, 36
  digital, 42
  winners', 22
  writing, 25

R. Goizueta Business & Society Institute, 138
ripple effect, of influence, 34
Roosevelt, Anna, 78
Rotary Global Grant, 167, 168

S

Sabet, Mona, 33–35
safety schools, 4, 14
Safi, Basil, 41
Sail to Scale, 33
salary, 155, 157
  higher-than-average, 155
sales pitch emails, 34
Santarsiero, Rachel, 77–79, 93
SAT score, 3–4, 154
  for Ivy League contender, 4
scholarships, 192
selection committee, 2, 11, 37, 86
  Cornell, 5–6
  insider information, 4
  and urgency, 92
selector
  "double whammy" question to, 46–48
  empathy, 177
  follow-up thank-you email to, 48
  LinkedIn connection, 48
  selection process, 45
  self-introduction to, 43–48
  winner's mindset, 171
self-centric need, 65

self-confidence, 13, 18, 19, 49, 168, 170–172, 179
self-doubt, 7, 177
self-introduction, 34, 39
  to selector, 43–48
self-praise, 173, 175, 176
Serrano, Camille, 93, 95
Shark Tank, 15, 97–99
skills, 8
  communication, 8
  interview, 80, 81
  storytelling, 5
social media, 19
Society, Technology, and Policy Program (STP), 79
speaker, 196, 214, 215
  persuasive, 26
speaking, 175
  as skill, 8
specificity, 124, 142
spray and pray approach, 9
Squatty Potty, 99
stakeholder engagement, 72
Stanford University, 17, 103
stickiness, 34, 38, 46, 55, 130
storytelling, 5
  communication and, 26
  methods, 54
  to online training course, 54
  skills, 5, 7
story "hook" (*see* "hook" story)
student-led organization on-site volunteer services, 60

student loan debt, 155
success and failure, as opportunities, 10
Sullivan, Jack, 113
Syracuse University, 3

T
tall poppy syndrome, 175
Tatkon Center, 42
Tech Stars, 104
TED talks, 9
Tesla, 67
timeliness, 85
   in application, 87
   business investment, 88–91
   corporate job opening, 87
   government/nonprofit job opening, 87
   graduate school, 88
   in organization, 86–87
   project proposal, 89–91
   through urgency, 92–96
tone, 147, 153, 169
trust, 16, 39, 61, 169, 170

U
unique benefits, 101–102, 113–117
   of opportunity, 104
   organization, 112–118
   in pitch, 102
   school, 112

universities mission, 63
University of Alaska Center for Economic Development (UACED), 197
University of Delaware, 3
University of Kiel, 91
University of Massachusetts, 52
University of Michigan, 97
University of North Carolina—Chapel Hill (UNC), 113
urgency, 85
   into pitch, 93–96
   timeliness through, 92–96
U.S. Department of Education, 67
U.S. Foreign Service, 145

V
values statements, 68
   search online for, 81

W
Wang, Lauren, 17
website, 105
well-being, 13
Wharton Business School, 98
"*What I Learned from 100 Days of Rejection*" (Jiang 2016), 9
White, Sojourner, 49
William & Mary, 69

winner's mindset, 8, 170, 182, 183
   vs. competitors, 22
   development of, 22–25
   elegance, 171–173
   preparation with confidence, 2, 22
Worcester Polytechnic Institute, 78
words, specificity, 127–128
World Trade Center attacks (9/11), 89, 120

WPI Development Design Lab, 79
writer's block, 21
writing, 129
   personal pitch, 25–26
   persuasive, 80
   persuasive story in, 26

Y

Y Combinator (YC), 97, 100, 104

Z

Zechmeister, Elizabeth, 44, 45